Cooking in the Deep-South with Chef Bob

By

Sir Robert "Chef Bob" Vaningan O.S.C.

It's Easy! Chef Bob 2003!

This book is a work of non-fiction. Some names and places were changed to protect the privacy of those individuals. The events and situations are true.

ISBN: 1-4033-9282-X (e-book)
ISBN: 1-4033-9283-8 (Softcover)
ISBN: 1-4033-9284-6 (Hardcover)

Library of Congress Control Number: 2002095574

This book is printed on acid free paper.

Printed in the United States of America
Bloomington, IN

Photo on cover by Barry Altmark© copyright 2003
Back cover Natalie Carr© copyright 2003
Food styling and photos Robert Richard Vaningan© copyright 2003

1stBooks - rev. 05/09/03

Acknowledgements

There are probably a thousand people I would like to acknowledge for helping me in one way or another. **Cooking in the Deep-South** was a concept requested by His Royal Highness, Prince Ambroise Dolgrouky d` Anjou. His Eminence said, "You have the knowledge, now write it down." Thank you your Highness.

Thank you to His Grace, Bishop James A. Gaines and Reverend Rosemarie Gaines, two people who really love people. Thanks Admiral Larson, United States Naval Academy, and Lieutenant Dan. Mr. Newt Gingrich for your encouraging words. Julie Nixon Isenhower for the party. The White House Presidential Culinary Team for a behind the scenes, four hour tour. Carl Nordberg, and my Deep-South culinary team, George White, Jack Prater, Doug Bryant and Brad Peters. Janie Green for being the beginning of something great. Billie Odom for your continued love and homegrown tomatoes. Stan Derencin for your guidance in the early years and now.

Andy Camardella, for being my friend and culinary Yoda. Kathy Camardella for your helpful ideas. Ken McKnielly the Master, who took me as a know nothing apprentice, teaching me the art of galantines for competitions and requiring me to play chess on the line during the rush, to teach me speed and style. Richard Bishop, who's emotional passion lit the flames of many. I will never forget when I was a youngling and asked you, "What kind of Chef are you; executive chef, sous-chef, or chef de cuisine?" and you replied, "I am a F****** cook!" Thank you Chef, I do not cook without thinking of you. Alonzo Brown, grill sergeant, John Randaza for showing me what seafood is supposed to be. Richard Carpenter, who's teachings I use every day. Steven Freeman, Sylvester "Sly", Chef Walter Delane salt and pepper, Chef Diane, Mary, one of the best sauté people I've ever met. Chef Tomas, chef to the Prince of Saudi Arabia for letting me cook with you those two weeks. Thomas Williams, the poet. Miss Mildred, and Sam. Willie McGhee, art culinaire incarnated. Harry Piecesses, Casey Singledom, Michele Bouit, Herman Rouche, for making me compete. Michele` Delcrose, Keith Keough, Spud Rae, and Tim Ryan for the great critics. Chef John Folse for inspiring every Chef-owner worldwide. Chef Clayton Sherrod, for helping me step up. Coby Morgan and Ron "Hap" Kotter. Frank Stitt for being so kind and setting a standard for all of us to cook better. Chris Dupont for all the fun, Archie from Springville, Scott and Carla, sous-chefs in training. L.S.U. Twins Marie and Michelle, thank you girls. Cindy and Harry Sloan. Chef C.L.E. in the N.C. The McCowans. The OLE Springville Bakery Crew. "Little Chris Sanders" for the 1000's of pounds of cake, cookie, and brownie batter late at night. Caleb Keith, I'll never forget what you did for me, we miss you. Pam and Eddy. Bill Jr., Buddy Whitworth and Mike, for the real Mexican cooking lessons. Myra Boone for the help and the great Cinco party every year. Miss Ruby for your hard life, beautiful personality, and fried chicken. Alfreedia, Met, Sandra and Patricia, for teaching me about your world. Sidney Cowan, Lakeview Crescent, Willie Mae Cowan. Jeff "Bad Foots" Johnson and big Mark. Pam and Terry Gallagher for adopting my family into yours. I hope you know how much you mean to me. Chef Diamond Dave. Les Cunningham, the idea bank. Jim Kinney for the love of food.

Laurent Manrique, Daniel Boulud, Claude Troigros, Henry Meer, Sulivan Portay, Jacque Torres, Francoise Payard, and Scott Hoyland, for allowing me in your kitchens, teaching me greatness, and treating me like royalty. Thank you Jeremiah Towers, whom I've never met, for inspiring me when I was an apprentice, I think of food differently because of you. Chef Anthony Bourdain for your literary works of culinary thought. Thank you great chefs, I think of you all when I plate up at night.

Dixie Store Fixtures, the Cypress Family, for helping my restaurants grow. Butch Evans, Evan's meats, thanks for years of the best-farmed meats. Mike Piazza, the Wrights, and the Cheney family, especially Edith. The Weavers, and the Corrs. Jerry Jones, ducks unlimited. R. L. Shrieber for perfect herbs, spices, and nuts every month.

On a personal level there are about half a million people that I would love to acknowledge, Mr. Elie my fifth grade teacher for bringing reading into my life. Steve Fredrick. Pastor Paul for loving me and showing me the love of God. The old Norwegian man Clarence, who taught me how to run a trap line and field dress a rabbit. Chris Hardie, my old friend. Uncle Bob Vaningan, for that summer in Atlanta, my first symphony, and for introducing me to fine dining at 15. Joyce Gilmore for helping me proofread and for not letting me quit High school, I love you. Are you ready for the next book? Mrs. Dunner for loving my spirit, and the prayers. Mr. Davenport (Huffman High) for the hard licks. Connie Brimmer for your listening ear in class. The Duckets, the Perry family, Mama and Papa Reese, Dan Ronsisvallie, Paul Perry and Carry Thompkins for keeping me on the straight and narrow.

My very dear Brenda and Randal Wilks. Billy, George and Linda Reed for the great homegrown vegetables and the freshest fish. Bill Whitworth, brother Cecile, and Pastor Andy. Dr. Sosnowchick and Shelbie. Dr. McKlenny and family. Frank Battles, the preacher. James Warren, a man who truly walks hand in hand with God. Randy and Libby, an example of love thy neighbor. Sister Sarah, thank you for all the home cooked meals you brought to us. The Marquez family, I will always cherish the time we had, I love you. Misty, thanks for your pastry love. David Tanner, my civilian sous-chef and friend. My crew at our restaurant The Chocolate Cottage, Ovada, Lisa, and the Chef Bob Catering Team, I couldn't do it with out you. Every customer that has patronized my restaurants.

The beautiful brides that allowed me to be a permanent part of their lives. WBRC Fox 6 General Manager Dennis Leonard, Janice Rogers, Rick Journey, Bill Bolen, Sarah Verser and Mickey Ferguson, Randy Mize and all the technical and visual crew at Good Day Alabama. Joe. Producers, Suzanne Cornet and crew. My accountant and my attorney, many thanks. Every line cook I have ever worked with, you inspired me. Jim Miller, Herb (Mac Daddy), my former sous-chef Levy Sanders, Miss Faye, Terry, and Mary. Ron and Liz Moore, for getting me started. Chris "Nick" Nicholson for your beautiful spirit. Guido and Simona for helping my business grow. Joe Yarbrough, for making me do it on my own. Bonnie Tidwell, thank you for believing in me. Wayne and Faye Payne for all the great nights of sanctuary at Roses and Lace Bed and Breakfast in Ashville, Alabama. Evelyn and Don. Prudence Hillburn thanks for your guidance, Nick Malgieri for the inspiring words and e-mails. Jeff Smith, (Frug) for your life and professional works. Sharon and Larry Pierce, thank you. Robbie Griffith for being my friend all these years, the crazy days of our youth, taking care of me sometimes, chocolate oatmeal cookies, cooking with me for the Christmas parties, and the scuba diving trips.

My cousin Bert for fixing the technical problems, and idea board bouncer, I love you brother.

My parents, my siblings, Rod, Rayna, and Randee. My nieces and nephews, all my cousins, aunts and uncles, especially Cathy and Celeste, uncle Tom and aunt Jane for the help and advice. George, Mattie and Richard, we miss you. Rob Wait for the gumbo lessons.

Thanks to the best line cook I have ever had the pleasure of cooking with, my son Richard, who began cooking when he was just four years old and tested most of the recipes in this book. He is going to be one of the great ones, his passion and his creativity are unique, his love of cooking is pure, his life is destined for greatness, thank you son, I love you. My daughter Angela, who is very passionate about our customers and one of the best public relations people I know, she gets it from her mother. Her genuine love for people will take her far in this life. Live life to the fullest my sweetheart, and in pleasing others, don't forget about your dreams and about your own happiness. I love you, see you in Australia. Nathan my son, I love you. I am very proud to be your dad. You will achieve your goals, just do it. Life is short so make everyday count. Don't give up too quickly, greatness takes time. Morgan, our youngest, who wants to be the best at everything. I hope all that you have dreamed and planned come true, I love you. To my wife Lady Darlene, who is more beautiful now than the first moment I saw her and fell deeply in love. Thank you for being the foundation of love and stability for all these years and being the perfect helpmate and conjoining soul mate, I love you then, now, and always. My grandmother Mama Payne, a corner stone of my life and a woman of soft-spoken southern, elegance.

Finally, my grandfather John C. Hooper (Papa John), WWII veteran and lover of life, cooking, and the coast. He took me in as a troubled teen and made me a man. What I am today, I owe to him. This book is dedicated to him, thank you Papa John, for everything.

I miss you.

Table of Contents

Geo. Hyde,

ROVING RAMBLERS—Seated, Earl and Marston, standing, Slim, Jess, Lefty, Burt, Chuck and Roland. Over WSGN, 6:00 A.M., Saturday, 1:00 P.M.

Introduction

The words "Deep South Cuisine" are often misunderstood. Not to be confused with Cajun or Creole, which is strictly Louisiana, Deep South Cuisine is instead the product of the whole Southern culture, with hospitality and soul food. In writing this book, it is my intention to define Deep South cooking as a regional cuisine and dispense with the cliché, that everything in the Deep South is fried. Well, there is a good bit of that, but there is so much more, as you are about to discover. First of all, the Deep South consists of those states below the Mason-Dixon line with the exception of Louisiana, Texas, and Florida. Louisiana is a culinary world of its own, different from anywhere else on Earth. Texas is southwestern style all the way, and Florida is as far away from Deep South Cuisine as Canada.

Secondly, Deep South cooking is deeply rooted in long-practiced traditions, and is as much a part of the culture of the region as wine is to France. A descendent of share cropping settlers and Cherokee blood, I grew up in the Deep South living on crispy fried green tomatoes, black-eyed peas, okra, turnip greens, creamy grits, hot buttered corn bread, fluffy biscuits and saw mill gravy, the most mouth watering fried chicken you have ever encountered, just picked ripe peaches made into cobbler, and I'll never forget the homemade ice cream.

I want to give you a chance to escape into my world, the Deep South. Although it is a subject that covers many different styles and cultures, my mission is simple; to teach Deep South cooking using my experience as a chef, and give you a unique insight into producing creative meals for your family and friends. Y'all enjoy.

A Chef's Food Memories

I grew up in the Deep South with sounds of guitars, fiddles and banjos, playing late into the evenings. My grandfather (Daddy Bert) was a steel worker and the leader of a country gospel band that usually played somewhere every weekend. The Deep South way of life is to work hard, love God and family, cook with soul giving love and respect for the food and the people you are cooking for.

My earliest memory of food preparation is my grandmother (Mama Payne) preparing apple and cheese cubes lanced with toothpicks and arranged ever so carefully on a small, decorative plate and presented to me after a long, hard day of kindergarten. I thought about that beautiful fruit and cheese platter all day. On my way home, remembering abc's and 2 plus 2, my taste buds began to anticipate the tart apples, peeled and cubed, nestled beside yellow cheddar, then lanced with colored tooth picks and three or four crackers fanned on the side of the cartooned plate. Tune the black and white television to Mr. Rodger's and I felt like the President of the free world with my gourmet feast on my tiny throne.

I remember the day that I learned Deep South cooking was about love and appreciation. It was the day my dad came home from the Vietnam War. My mother, grandmother and all of my aunts worked for two days preparing the perfect Deep South, welcome home, grand gastronomic feast. It was like something from the movies, everything southern and everything edible was presented that evening. I spent most Sunday's as a child going to Sunday school or visiting relatives.

When you visit relatives on Sunday in the Deep South, somebody's cooking something great. I remember at my Aunt Kitty Koise's (we called her that because as little children we couldn't pronounce Lillie Loise) humble house, we would have races to the barn and back as Sunday dinner was being prepared. Later, I learned that the races were designed to keep kids out of the kitchen and increase our appetite. When it was time to eat, someone would make a whooping sound, and we would run to the creaking, old screen door and line up to wash our hands. It was hot in that little house in the summer, air conditioned by a single, oscillating fan. We didn't care, we knew how good it was going to be.

On the 1940's style kitchen table were stacks of fried green tomatoes, big ceramic bowls of crispy, popcorn style, fried okra, colossal platters of Deep-South fried chicken, coal black skillets of golden browned corn bread, plenty of home spun honey, jams, jellies, real butter, glass pitchers of candy sweet iced tea, and at least two different kinds of cakes and two or three different pies. My other Aunt, Elise (aunt E) was also quite the cook. As with most southerners with more than a hand full of dirt, there was a garden.

Big platters of sliced juicy, ripe, red tomatoes, pots of greens and black-eyed peas, mile high biscuits, washtub size bowls of potato salad, fried pies and homemade ice cream. Aunt E's house was more sophisticated, with all Victorian-decor, hard wood floors, and air conditioning. Still, the food was the same, heart loved, southern, and soulful.

My parents were quite resourceful, manning a garden, raising chickens, pigs and a calf every year. Trapping and hunting every season. It was truly a building block for my future chef life, as a young boy, learning first hand that chickens, sausage, steaks and vegetables didn't magically grow at the supermarket, but were labored over to provide wonderful tasting and celebratory foods. I don't remember ever going to the grocery store that much. I also have a permanent picture in my mind of my mother creating everything from scratch for our small crowd. I can still see and smell, the cookies cooling on wire racks, baked apple or rhubarb pies with the most incredible crust made with actual lard from our actual pig, and five or six perfectly baked loaves of bread. My mother sliced homemade bread for our school lunches.

My grandfather came from a food family who sold produce and chickens to the chef of the famed Biltmore House in North Carolina. Mr. Hooper (great grandfather) made enough money to move his family to the Magic City, Birmingham, Alabama, where my grandfather Papa John was raised. My great grandfather opened the first white tablecloth cafe in Birmingham, the famed Hooper's Cafe. The special of the house was a salad; a twenty-four ounce T-bone, baked potato, and biscuits, all for thirty-five cents, tip not included. After the death of his father, the closing of Hooper's Cafe, and the end of World War II, my grandfather, Papa John became a conductor for Southern Railroad. He loved the railroad, but his true love was cooking. Coming from a food family Papa John did most of the cooking. He always had a huge garden every year, and even though I didn't like working in it, there is nothing in this world that will compare to picking a basket of vegetables, cleaning, cooking, and eating them, all in a matter of hours. It is an event to me, to catch fish, prepare them that evening and take a flashlight into the garden, searching for that perfect, ripe tomato, still warm from the sun. I would pick it from the vine, smell the ripe tomato perfume and take a huge bite like I would with an apple. Next I reached into my back pocket, retrieving a salt shaker, and in a private ceremonial ritual, I would throw the salt into the air and catch it with the tomato, then take another bite. I soon realize I still had to pick some tomatoes for dinner. I learned the basics from Papa John. First, learning how to pull weeds, plant and grow the most beautiful vegetables. I remember Papa John would stop working in the middle of the garden and say "looka hee-uh boya", taking a perfect red tomato specimen from the dark green vine. He would reach into his back pocket and retrieve his razor sharp buck knife, cut 5 or 6 slices and fan them out on his arm. He would then reach into his other back pocket for a shaker of salt, season the slices and offer me some from his dark, tanned, leather-like arm platter. I have never had a better tasting slice of tomato. It must have been the combination of the scorching Alabama sun, the perfect ripe tomato, salted on one side and on the other side absorbing the essence of an old rail road man who loved me so much.

He took great care and effort planting, picking, cooking, freezing, canning and preserving his labor of love. And it was a beautiful happening to watch him give it away with such joy. I really miss him since his death in March of 1995. This book is dedicated to him. Thank you Papa John, for everything. I miss you.

Road to the White House

I was born in Birmingham, Alabama and began real cooking when I was 15. I knew nothing. My grandfather Papa John taught me the home cooking basics, fresh vegetables, soups and stews, fried fish, steaks, BBQ chicken and smoked pork, canning and freezing. I landed a job at a local all you can eat buffet house, washing pots and pans. I didn't have enough experience to run the big dish machine so I got the glamour job of pot washer. I wouldn't change that experience for anything. I moved up to chef's assistant, sounds good, but it really meant chef's runner. It was my first time to see a chef up close and personal. His name was George and he loved to cook. He would sing all morning, mostly old spiritual songs. It made me very happy to be there, just the chef and me. He would allow me stir his pots for him, and to me, I was cooking. I would go to work at 5:00 am and help chef George till 7:30am and then ride my motorcycle to school. I would return to work at 4:00 and work until 9:00pm. I loved it. I couldn't wait to get up in the mornings. Chef would let me off work if I had to do a lot of schoolwork, but that was rare. I worked in several other restaurants, a Mexican restaurant, a steak house, and a diner. I worked at a pizza chain where I met my soul mate Darlene. I love her more now than I did then. I started nursing school so I could make the big bucks and support my family. I didn't like it.

I was working at a nursing home and a chef appeared on television. Every time a chef was on television I wrote the recipe down and made it at home. The chef's name was James Ready. He said the first chef school in Alabama would begin in 30 days, my heart pounded faster as I listened, I couldn't think of anything else that day. I told my wife I wanted to go to chef school and she said go for it! I called chef Ready and he told me to see chef McKnielly at the Wynfrey hotel. I went to the 4 star hotel that was still under construction, ignored the signs that said no applications accepted today, and told them Chef Ready sent me here from the American Culinary Federation. It was like my granddaddy always said, "It is who you know". They took me directly to the chef. In the unfinished kitchen there was a long line of future employees being interviewed by the chef. I was taken in front of the line and was introduced as, a guy from the American Culinary federation. The chef got up, shook hands and told the interviewees he would be back in15 or 20 minutes. We went down stairs to what later became an employee cafeteria. Chef McKnielly was quite the gentleman. He made coffee for both of us, sat down and said, "So, what is your specialty? Banquets, Garde' Manger, fine dinning? How long have you been a chef?" I was embarrassed. I told him there must have been a misunderstanding. I wanted to learn to be a chef. He laughed and said "well you made it this far, I guess I could take on an apprentice." I knew this was the beginning of something great. I was taught all the basics as an apprentice chef. There I was in a brand new 4 star property that had every amenity. Every thing was made from scratch, veal stocks, chicken stocks, dressings and sauces. This was a culinary wonderland. I would work my shift, clock out and return to work on my own time, to learn. Chef McKnielly took lots of time teaching me galantines, aspic work; grand buffet preparation, butchering, ice sculpture, and would constantly test me on **Le Repertoire de la Cuisine** by Louis Saulnier and Edouard Brunet. He would also make me play chess during the rush to teach speed and organization. I don't think I ever won a game, but what I did learn I still use today.

The first, very famous chef I met was Chef John Flose. It was like meeting the Michael Jordan of the chef world. He had it all together, a love for God, two restaurants, television, cookbooks, traveling the world teaching his Louisiana Cuisine and still had time to spend talking to me about being an apprentice. That was it. I knew I was where I belonged.

I eventually competed as a chef in a world class cooking competition in Chicago while I was still an apprentice, which I placed 3rd, bronze medal. Chefs from all over the world were there, Great Britain, Japan, Canada, South America and many from the United States. I certainly didn't think I had a chance. Imagine how humbling and proud I felt when the judges placed a bronze medal indicator on my table. The Great Britain team came over to talk to me because they thought I was from Birmingham, England. I think they were disappointed.

After two years I was allowed to write the menu for the fine dining restaurant and take charge of the kitchen when the chef was off. You have to imagine, at that point I thought I was the greatest chef in the world! I soon found out how little I knew, when I took my first chef job at a Birmingham city club and didn't know how much meat to order for 350 people, or how much dressing to make for 500 people. I had to call my mentors and ask for their help, and without telling me I told you that you weren't ready, they helped, even came to my new job and helped. To this day I still love to learn. I want to learn something new about cooking everyday I am alive.

My passion for cooking became stronger with every new chef job. I eventually became executive chef at a country club where I was allowed the freedom to create my own style of cuisine. While I was there I was noticed nationally several times in magazines and news articles. I competed in national competitions as well as local. One day the phone rang for me and I was very busy with my hand in chocolate. I took the call. It was Chef Laurent Manrique from Peacock Alley restaurant at the Waldorf-Astoria hotel in New York. He simply asked me if I would like to come to New York for a chef tour and learning experience. I of course said yes. While I was there I was treated like royalty. Every kitchen I worked in received me with open arms. Chef Henry Meer, the Cub room, Chef Claude Troigros, C.T.'s Chef Portay

Le Cirque, Chef Daniel Boulud, Restaurant Daniel and Chef Laurent Manrique, Peacock Alley. The whole trip was started by a conversation between my wife's uncle, Bishop James A. Gaines and His Royal Highness Prince Ambrose Dolgrouky d' Anjou in New York. His Highness is a fan of chefs who have a passion for God and cooking. My wife's uncle told His Highness about my cooking career and The Royal Prince asked the Chef of Peacock Alley to invite me up. I met His Highness and He asked me intense questions about my faith in GOD and my cooking experience.

Each restaurant I worked in, the royal family dined and I assisted in preparing their foods. My wife was picked up every night by Royal limo and joined the Royal family for dinner. I rode the subway everyday into Manhattan to Park and 50th, the Waldorf-Astoria, and had espresso with chef Manrique every morning before taking a cab to one of the top-flight restaurants, where I would work until 11:00 or 12:00 midnight before heading back on the subway. I would start all over at 5:00am. My time in each restaurant I owe to Chef Laurent Manrique, who coordinated with the chefs in New York to allow a stage in their kitchens. Thank you Laurent Manrique.

After working a stage in each restaurant I was asked to dine with the Royal family in the private dinning room at Peacock-Alley restaurant. I walked into the private dinning room and the only empty chair was at the head of the table where I was seated. Menus were propped upright and were custom made for this special evening. The top of the menu read His Most Eminent Royal Highness confers Knighthood on Robert "Chef Bob" Vaningan by the Order of Saint Catherine. I have never been so penitent. I certainly did not feel worthy of such a title. My wife Darlene was knighted Lady Darlene Vaningan by the Order of Chevalier of Sinai. Darlene has always been a lady, but now carries the title Lady Darlene. The food was stellar and the service impeccable, we each had our own waiter. After dinner and the most stimulating conversation I have ever had, His Royal Highness commanded me to kneel before him. In total humbleness I kneeled and His Highness's cousin Prince Robert from Malta, pulled the 700 year old sword from its sheath and touched it to my shoulders saying "In the name of the Father, the Son, and the Holy Spirit, I dub the Sir Robert "Chef Bob" Vaningan by the Order of Saint Catherine and Royal House d' Anjou." Next was my wife Darlene. "Arise Sir Robert and Lady Darlene." We were so reverent.

His Highness called for a toast. It was a very large, hand blown, paper-thin glass and in it a rare brandy. Described by His Royal Highness as a taste of history, for tonight we drink a toast to Sir Robert "Chef Bob" and Lady Darlene. In the glass was a special private reserve of Louis XIII brandy. The next morning the staff at the Waldorf-Astoria greeted us as Sir Robert and Lady Darlene.

Soon after that a food writer from **Chef Magazine** called to ask me about cooking in the deep south. He wrote a great article about southern cooking. Chef Nordberg, the food writer was part of a special Naval Academy detail to find regional cooks and bring them to Annapolis, Maryland to teach authentic cuisine from four regions of the United States. I was asked, you guessed it, to lead the Deep-South Team. It was the Navy's 220th Birthday so we went all out with ice sculptures and everything southern. The menu; Whole Smoked wild boar with black strap molasses, turnip greens and black-eyed peas, grits, corn pones, pecan pie, sweet potato pie and the birthday cake, white chocolate pound cake with battleship gray icing and marzipan battle ships. It was a lot of work, but a lot of fun.

As a thank you, the Navy gave us V.I.P. seating at the Blue Angels air show. We were seated with Robert Shuller (he and I had a great conversation) James Earl Jones, Ron Howard, and Tom Selec. The Navy also sent us to The White House for a security cleared, private, behind the scene tour. No words can describe it. I saw President Clinton's lunch being prepared. Whole-wheat pasta with chicken and tomato sauce. They let us call our wives from a white house phone, and the President was supposed to come meet us, but I think he was interviewing an intern while we were there. We saw the secret service kitchen, met the first family's chef and stood at the press podium. I was allowed to see the Oval Office, I cried. All the patriotism in my body welled up and came out of my eyes. I was just a cook from Birmingham, Alabama who loves what he does with a passion, and there I was, a knight in the White House, being honored as a dignitary.

Eventually I opened my own bakery and catering business. Years after that I opened a restaurant called The Chocolate Cottage, where I use all I have learned and where I can cook and train others, and work with my family as GOD intended.

I am currently working on a new restaurant.

Visit me at www.chefbob.com

Love God, Family, and The Deep South.
Sir Robert "Chef Bob" Vaningan O.S.C.

Nous, Ambroise, par la Grace de Dieu Archevêque, et par le droit dynastique, Prince Dolgorouky et Duc Grand de Volynia, Roi de Cherwona-Rus et de Halich, Prince Régent d'Anjou et de Bourbon-Condé, Prince de Naples et de Czern Csernohorsky, Duc d'Isle de Ste Clément, envoyons nos salutati à tous ceux à qui ces présentes peuvent arriver.

Attendu que, Nous, dans l'exercice de nos prérogatives et de no droits souverains, et conformément à notre volonté souveraine, établissons ces lettres patentes, et par la décrétons et conférons sur

Robert Chef Bob Vaningan

l'état le plus honorable de la chevalerie dans notre le plus royale et noble

l'Ordre de Ste. Catherine

avec le grade et le rang de :

Chevalier

— et Chef de la Maison Royale de France et d'Anjou de Naple

Par conséquent, de plus, Nous chargeons le même d'accomplir loyalement toutes les responsabilités qui lui incombent avec cet honneur; et de jouir de tous les droits, les honneurs et les privilèges selon les anciennes traditions de la chevalerie chrétienne et de notre maison la plus royale.

Son Altesse Royale, Ambroise Dolgorouky d'Anjou

Greffier

Date: June 10, 1993

Chancelier

+ Chev. Eugene

Dimitri

APRÈS AVOIR OUI NOTRE CONSEIL
DE L'ORDRE DES CHEVALIERS DU SINAI

Vu la Bulle d'Or de l'Empereur Justinien :
Vu les droits et privilèges conférés à l'Ordre des Chevaliers du SINAI ;
L.L.M.M. Impériales les Empereurs Grecs et Latins de Constantinop
Vu les décrets de L.L.M.M. les Rois de Jérusalem :
Vu les décrets et les Bulles de N.N.S.S. les Pontifes Romains ;
Vu la Volonté de S.A.R. Monseigneur ABBAS HILMI II Khédive e
Vu les us et coutumes et les droits y afférant ;
Vu les privilèges des charges que nous assumons.

Nous conférons à

Darlene Vaningan

le titre de

Dame

Avons Admis et Reçu dans l'ORDRE des CHEVALIERS du SI

Au nom du GRAND MAÎTRE

Admettons et recevons aux conditions portées par les Statuts avec tous
Droits et Privilèges attachés à la dite qualité.

En foi de quoi nous avons scellé et signé les présentes pour valoir ce que de dr

puisse justifier de son admission dans Notre Ordre et jouir partout où il sera
Honneurs, Droits, Prérogatives, Privilèges, Immunités, etc... accordés par
Seigneurs et dont jouissent et doivent jouir tous les Nobles Chevaliers

Le Grand Connétable   Le Lieutenant-Général   L'Archi-C

registre et scellé des Armes de l'Ordre   par Nous   et   de l'an de g

Road to the White House

Chef Bob gets knighted

Laurent Manrigue, Prince Dologrouky d'Anjou and
Prince Robert of Malta.

Chapter 1
Southern Breads

Chapter-One

Southern Bread

True Deep-South Southerners take pride in their breads. Bread is a large part of southern cuisine. It would not be considered proper to serve a southern cooked meal with out the accompaniment of at least one type of southern bread. American Indians introduced early settlers to maize, or corn, and cooks of the early years learned to cook a stiff corn mush, like today's grits or polenta. Hoecakes were one of the first "corn breads" to appear in the south. Invented and perfected by African slaves who created culinary magic out of virtually nothing. Stone ground cornmeal, salt, boiling water, and a little oil is all that is needed. Of course, you needed a fire and a good garden hoe. Hoecakes, as indicated by the name, were cooked on garden hoes. I personally think you can make a great hoecake in an old-fashioned iron skillet. I speculate manipulating thick batter and shaping it into the palm of their hand and frying the football shaped bread invented corn pones.

Heartshorn (ground deer antlers) was used as a type of baking soda since medieval times. Corn bread became ever more popular with the addition of milled flour, production of baking powder, baking soda, buttermilk, and addition of eggs, made a more cake-like bread. Bread is a natural and wonderful thing. Yeast lives in the air and on wheat kernels. Cultivation of yeast dates back about 5,000 years or more, with the Egyptians building huge bakeries to make bread for 20,000 to 30,000 people every day. That might take a couple of batches. All you have to do to cultivate yeast is to mix wheat flour with water, then the yeast begins to feed and grow.

The Holy Bible mentions bread many times when talking about food or life. Bread is the staff of life. I was ever so humbled to learn that Bethlehem translated means House of Bread. Jesus is called the bread of life and Mathew 4:4 reads "Man cannot live by bread alone, but by every word that proceeds out of the mouth of God." Jesus used bread to symbolize His body at the Last Supper. WOW! These thoughts go through my mind when I am making, baking, or eating bread. I wrote the bread chapter first because bread is my favorite thing to make, and if you are making yeast bread, you may need to let the bread rise while you prepare the remainder of your great Deep South meal. Do not be afraid to try all the bread recipes. I wrote the recipes simply, so you can produce southern bread at it's finest. An important note is to use freshly milled corn meal and flour and store in airtight containers and or freezer. Relax, have fun, break bread, give thanks, and enjoy with someone you love.

Pecan Onion Toast

Hoecakes

I speculate that hoecakes were descendents of Johnny cakes, that were descendents of journey cakes, that were descendents of Shawnee cakes, a corn meal mush wrapped in wet cabbage leaves and laid in fire coals, then packed in leather skins for travel, or journeys. Make in pancake shape, but thin and crispy.

2 cups white corn meal

3 Tablespoons corn oil

1 teaspoon salt

1 cup boiling water

¼ to ½ cup corn oil for frying

Blend the corn meal and salt in a medium sized mixing bowl. Make a well in the center and add the 3 Tablespoons of oil and the 1-cup of boiling water. With a large spoon, mix in a folding motion until a fairly smooth batter is achieved. Place some of the 1/4-1/2 cup of oil in a 10-inch iron skillet. Heat oil for about 3 minutes on medium high heat. When oil is hot, pour about 1/2 cup of hoecake batter into heated oil and cook about 2-3 minutes per side. Repeat until all batter is used. Keep warm wrapped in a towel.

Corn Pones

Corn pones are defined differently according to who is giving the definition. Pone seems to be an English translation of a Native American word meaning small corn cake. Such a simple recipe, yet a difficult technique. It takes a little practice but you should come up with a crispy, brown, football shape, with a soft, grits-like center. Miss Alfreedia's corn pones were like large pancakes, made like hoecakes. She always said, "Boy, you want me make you a pone?"

2 cups white corn meal

1 cup flour (plain)

1 teaspoon salt

¼ cup corn oil plus extra oil for baking pan

¾ cup boiling water

1 cup boiling water

Blend corn meal, flour, and salt in a medium mixing bowl and make a well in the center. Add 1/4 cup of oil and 3/4 cup boiling water to center of well. With a large spoon drag dry mixture from outer edge, down and up through center of well. Continue in this folding motion. Bring the remaining 1 cup of water to a boil and this time pour the hot water around the outer edge and continue in the folding motion. Shape into egg size footballs using two large spoons, dipped in hot water, and place on a generously oiled sheet pan or large skillet and bake at 425° for 10 minutes, then turn down oven to 350° for an additional 15-20 minutes.

Plain Corn Bread

Some southerners will not deviate from a very humble corn bread recipe. And most southerners would have a heart attack if you added a little sugar in the recipe. Some will say, "It aint cornbread if its got sugar in it." Try all of the bread recipes in this chapter and find your favorite.

1 cup yellow corn meal (plain)

½ cup plain flour

1 teaspoon salt

¼ cup corn oil

1 cup boiling water

4 Tablespoons corn oil

Mix first five ingredients until fairly smooth. Place the 4 Tablespoons of corn oil in a 9-inch iron skillet. Heat skillet and oil in a preheated 425° oven for 10-15 minutes. Carefully take HOT skillet out of oven and scrape corn bread batter into hot skillet. Return to oven and bake for 30-40 minutes. Your result will be a thin, hard crusted, corn bread. Please be cautious with the HOT skillet.

Spoon Bread

We find spoon bread in the Carolinas and Virginia. Spoon bread is almost like a polenta pudding. This bread will grace your table for years and everyone will like having something new and different.

1 cup white corn meal

1 ½ teaspoons baking powder

½ teaspoon salt

2 eggs

3 Tablespoons butter (melted)

2 ¼ cups milk

Blend dry ingredients in a medium mixing bowl. In a sauce pot bring milk to a boil and slowly add dry ingredients into boiling milk while whisking vigorously. Cook while stirring continuously for 3-4 minutes. Take off heat and stir every 2-3 minutes for 15 minutes, allowing to cool slightly. Blend in the eggs and melted butter. Pour into a buttered, glass pie pan, or casserole dish. Bake at 425° for 30-40 minutes. Serve with a large spoon.

Bacon and Cheddar Spoon Bread

This spoon bread is tastier than the previous recipe with the addition of crisp bacon, cheddar cheese and garlic. It has been said that spoon bread was an invention from an accident. Someone added too many eggs and too much liquid to their corn bread recipe and rather than waste it, they baked it, and could only serve it with a spoon.

1 cup yellow corn meal (heaping)

2 cups water

2 cups sharp cheddar cheese (shredded)

1 stick butter (soft)

3 cloves garlic (chopped)

1 teaspoon salt

1 ¼ cup evaporated milk

4 eggs, separated

8 ounces bacon, fried crisp and crumbled

Mix corn meal and water in a pot over medium high heat. Stir continuously until mixture comes to a boil. Take off heat and stir in cheese, butter, garlic and salt. Add the milk, stir in egg yolks, add crisp, crumbled bacon. In a separate bowl with a wire whisk, or a mixer, whip the egg whites into stiff peaks. Fold in to spoon bread batter. Prepare a round or oval 2 quart casserole dish by buttering the bottom and sides, then dust lightly with dry bread crumbs. Scrape batter into dish and bake at 325° for 1 hour.

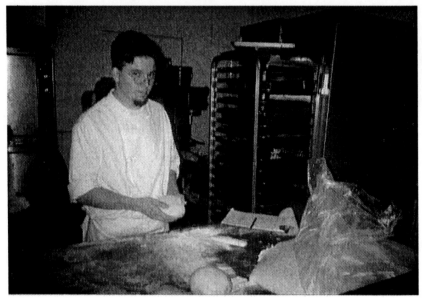

C.L.E.

Mattie's Corn Bread

Mattie was my wife's grandmother and this basic recipe comes out perfect most of the time, although she never had a problem making it. Some hints to help you are: Your iron skillet must be very seasoned. Your oven must be the correct temperature, the wind, humidity and barometric pressure must be... just kidding. Practice makes perfect.

1 ½ cups white corn meal

½ cup plain flour

2 teaspoons baking powder

1 teaspoon baking soda

½ teaspoon salt

4 Tablespoons mayonnaise

1 extra large egg

1 cup buttermilk

½ cup water

3 Tablespoons corn oil

Mix all ingredients, except corn oil, until fairly smooth and combined. Feel free to add a little water if batter seems too dry. Place the 3 Tablespoons of corn oil in a 9-inch iron skillet. Pour corn bread batter into skillet and bake at 425° for 35-45 minutes or until a wooden toothpick comes out clean. CAUTION: when you turn out corn bread on to a plate or platter be careful. Place plate on corn bread

Sir Robert "Chef Bob" Vaningan O.S.C.

then turn over with two hot pads; one on the plate bottom and one on the skillet handle. Turn over quickly, while praying the prayer of corn bread release. If it does not come out, you can always go rustic and just serve this great bread in the skillet! Place a folded towel on your table and set the iron skillet of bread on it. Serve in wedges like a piece of pie with lots of real butter!

Chef Bob's Favorite Corn Bread

This is my favorite corn bread recipe. It makes me think of my former sous-chef Levy. He used to bake this type of batter in buttered muffin tins. I prefer the trusted iron skillet. If you have trouble turning out the baked corn bread, just serve it still in the skillet. Place the hot pan on a folded towel so you don't burn your kitchen table. Slice into wedges and serve as you would a slice of pie. Use lots of real butter.

1 cup white cornmeal

½ cup plain flour

2 teaspoons baking powder

1 teaspoon baking soda

1 teaspoon salt

½ cup onions (chopped)

1 jalapeno (chopped)

½ cup whole kernal corn (frozen or canned)

4 Tablespoons mayonnaise

1 egg

1 cup buttermilk

4 Tablespoons corn oil

Sir Robert "Chef Bob" Vaningan O.S.C.

Mix all ingredients, except corn oil, in a medium mixing bowl and using a whisk, mix until a fairly smooth batter is obtained. Place 4 Tablespoons of corn oil into a 9-inch cast iron skillet. Pour corn bread batter into skillet and bake in a 450° preheated oven for 30-40 minutes or until a wooden toothpick inserted in the middle of the corn bread comes out clean.

Chef Bob's Hushpuppies

It has been said that hushpuppies were the hard crust particles floating in the fryer during a fish fry and the cook would throw these pieces to the dogs to keep them silent. I developed this recipe after trial and error. As for the puppy story, true or not you will be the king of the fish fry with these perfect hushpuppies.

2 ½ cups cornmeal

1 ½ cups plain flour

¼ cup sugar

1 teaspoon baking powder

1 teaspoon seasoned salt

1 teaspoon garlic powder

½ teaspoon baking soda

1 ½ pounds onions (chopped)

1 small tomato (chopped)

¾ cup corn

1 extra large egg

1 cup buttermilk

Mix all. Allow to stand at room temperature for 1 hour. Mix again, then refrigerate for at least 2 hours. Fry in clean oil at 325° use a little scoop. The secret is do not try to add more liquid to recipe. It will seem dry, but after it sits for an hour at room temperature and then at least 2 hours in the refrigerator, it will be perfect. Use peanut oil for best results. The secret to perfect frying is the temperature of the oil and very clean oil. Hushpuppies should be fried in a pot or fryer of it's own.

Yeast Biscuits

This is the biscuit recipe that any one can make. If you are unsure how to make Mattie's biscuits you will not have a problem making yeast biscuits.

4 ½ cups self-rising flour

1 teaspoon baking soda

1 teaspoon dry yeast

1 Tablespoon sugar

¾ cup corn oil

1 cup buttermilk (room temperature)

Sift dry ingredients into a medium mixing bowl and make a well in the center. Add oil and buttermilk to the well. Mix by hand until dough forms. Do not over mix. Roll dough out on floured surface and cut with a biscuit cutter. Place on buttered sheet pan or buttered iron skillets and allow biscuits to touch. Let biscuits rise for 1-2 hours in a warm place. Bake at 375°for 12-15 minutes.

Mattie's Biscuits

This recipe is one that must be mastered by practice. I know that Mattie used the same ceramic bowl, (that she made) of flour and never washed it. She made biscuits every day so the tiny bits of biscuit dough would be almost like a sour dough starter. I'm sure this is one of the great taste secrets that are created and learned after daily routine becomes second nature.

I remember staying with my aunt Rene for a couple of weeks one summer. She lived in the tiniest house I have ever seen. At 10 years old I could touch the ceiling, and to my surprise, there was no bathroom, and no shower. How was I going to take care of nature? There was an outhouse about 100 feet from the little abode. Nevertheless, aunt Rene made the best biscuits. She could only make a recipe for 4 individual, perfect biscuits. If she needed to make eight, she could not double the recipe. She said it just wouldn't turn out. So she would start over and make 4 more. Her four foot something frame and arthritic crooked hands, produced four of the best tasting biscuits I have ever tasted.

A friend of mine Miss Faye owns a bed and breakfast (Roses and Lace, Ashville, Alabama) and cooks her biscuits at 500° on buttered little iron skillets, then butters them again. WOW! Use this recipe as a guideline, but do not be afraid to try. Success comes from failure. Your hands are your greatest tools, so use them. If you want to protect your beautiful manicure and still be the perfect little biscuit maker, buy some latex exam gloves and dive in.

3 cups plain flour

1 heaping Tablespoon baking powder

1 teaspoon salt

½ teaspoon baking soda

½ cup shortening

1 ¼ cups buttermilk

4 cups plain flour

In a medium size bowl, sift the 3 cups of flour with the baking powder, salt, and baking soda. Use a pastry cutter or 2 knives and cut in the shortening until mixture is crumbly (pea like in size). With a fork or spoon, stir in the buttermilk to form a wet sticky mass. In a large bowl sift 4 cups of plain flour. Make a large well in the center and scrape the wet sticky mass into the center of the well. With your hand, fold in the flour a little at a time into the wet sticky mass. Be gentle. Turn dough over a few times as you work. You will not use all of the flour. What you are looking for is the dough to be very soft, but hold it's shape. With generously floured hands, pinch off about a golf ball size, or larger, piece of dough and roll in your hands. Do not over handle the dough. Over handling will make biscuits tough. Place on greased cake pans or cookie sheets. Pat down slightly and allow the biscuits to touch. Bake at 475° for 10-12 minutes. As soon as the biscuits come out, butter the tops.

Soft Rolls

One of my favorite breads is yeast bread. You will love the perfect rolls this recipe makes. You can also make "home loaves" basic white bread. I call it soft dough because the bread is so soft after baking.

5 ½ cups bread flour

½ cup sugar

1 Tablespoon salt

1 Tablespoon yeast

1 stick butter

1 egg

1 ½ cups milk

Warm milk to room temperature. Add all ingredients in a 5 quart mixer bowl with dough hook attachment. Mix for 10-12 minutes, or until dough is smooth and elastic. Lightly oil dough and place in a large, lightly oiled bowl. Cover with plastic wrap and allow to rise until double in bulk. Punch down dough and cut into golf ball sized pieces. Roll into tight shaped rolls and place on nonstick pan or parchment lined sheet pan and allow to rise until doubled. Bake at 350° for 10-12 minutes.

Buttermilk Cheese Bread

This recipe I developed for quick and easy preparation and guaranteed to rise. The buttermilk and cheese give body and tanginess to this bread. Use this bread to make grilled cheese, yum!

6 cups bread flour

2 teaspoons salt

1 Tablespoon baking powder

2 packages dry yeast

3 Tablespoons sugar

1 cup warm water

2 cups buttermilk

½ stick butter, melted

1 cup sharp cheese, shredded

In a mixer with dough hook add half of the flour, salt, baking powder, yeast, sugar, warm water, buttermilk, and butter. Mix for 2-3 minutes on medium speed. Scrape down sides of mixer bowl and continue to mix on low speed, adding flour a little at a time, until all the flour is used. Add the cheese and mix on medium speed until dough is smooth and elastic. Turn dough out onto a floured surface and cut into 2 equal pieces. Shape dough into a ball, tucking in underneath. Place in well greased bread pans or use non-stick. 9 inch by 5 inch pans. Allow to rise until doubled in size and bake in a 425° oven on bottom rack for 30-40 minutes. The bread will be browner than other breads because of the buttermilk. If it is browning too quickly, simply cover with foil.

Feather Bread

When I first began making bread I started with a recipe similar to this one. It is easy and produces a light (feather) crumb. This recipe makes 2 freeform loaves. Make this recipe with your hands, not a machine. You will get a more satisfying feeling, knowing you made it bread with your own two hands.

6 cups bread flour

1 Tablespoon salt

2 cups warm water

1 stick butter soft

2 Tablespoons sugar

2 packages yeast

2 Tablespoons plain cornmeal

1 egg white

In a large bowl add the flour and the salt. Make a well in the center, add the yeast, water, sugar and butter. Stir with a heavy duty spoon, incorporating the flour a little at a time. When dough comes together in a shaggy mass, begin using your hands. Keep your hands floured because this is a soft, sticky dough. Dust a work surface with flour and kneed dough for 8-10 minutes, adding more flour if needed. When dough is smooth and elastic, allow to rest for 10 minutes. Divide dough into 2 pieces. Roll each piece on a lightly floured surface into a rectangle, about 13 inch by 9 inch. Start from the long side and roll bread, pinching the dough into itself, until you have 2 nice log shaped loaves. Lightly oil a baking sheet and sprinkle with cornmeal. Place the loaves on the cornmeal and allow to rise. When bread has doubled in size, brush with egg white and place in a 425° oven for 30-40 minutes. I like to dip pieces of this bread into good, extra virgin olive oil and kosher salt.

Apple Bread

There are a surprising amount of apple orchards in the Deep South. In the Deep South we grow up eating **apple butter, apple pies, apple relish** (see index) and apple bread. Sounds like an apple supper. This is a fun and easy recipe to make and to give away as a gift. This bread is better the next day and freezes very well.

½ cup shortening

1 cup sugar

2 eggs

1 teaspoon vanilla

2 cups flour

1 teaspoon baking soda

½ teaspoon salt

3 Tablespoons buttermilk

2 cups peeled and diced apples

<u>Streusel Topping:</u>

2 Tablespoons shortening

½ teaspoon cinnamon

2 Tablespoons flour

2 Tablespoons sugar (rub topping ingredients together

with hands)

Cream shortening and sugar together until light and fluffy. Add eggs one at a time. Add vanilla. Sift dry ingredients and add. Add buttermilk and apples. Pour into greased 9x5x3 loaf pan. Sprinkle streusel over top and bake at 325° for 50-60 minutes. Cool for 15-20 minutes turn out on wire rack.

Banana Bread

I don't believe I have ever had a better tasting toast than a slice of banana bread, toasted and slathered with real butter. When you open your mouth to take a bite, your nostrils fill with a warm and sweet banana perfume, and then you bite down and a sudden rush of pleasure takes you where no toast has ever taken you before. This makes 2 loafs because you will discover as I did, one is not enough.

2 cups bread flour

2 cups cake flour

2 teaspoons baking soda

1 teaspoon salt

2 sticks of butter (melted)

2 cups of sugar

3 cups mashed, ripe bananas

1 cup of buttermilk

4 eggs

1 cup pecan pieces

Mix mashed bananas, melted butter, eggs, buttermilk and sugar in a large hand bowl. Sift flours, baking soda and salt into banana mixture. Mix until well blended. Fold in pecans. Pour batter into 2 buttered, 9x5x3 loaf pans. Bake at 340° for 45-55 minutes, or until a wooden toothpick inserted into the middle of the bread, comes out clean.

Gingerbread

Intended in the 16th century to be served as plain holiday bread, it is more like cake.

Eat this bread warm, with peach preserves and butter.

3 ½ cups flour

1 cup sugar

2 sticks butter

1 cup molasses or sorghum syrup

1 teaspoon salt

2 teaspoons baking soda

1 Tablespoon ground ginger

1 teaspoon cinnamon

1 teaspoon ground cloves

1 teaspoon ground nutmeg

4 eggs

2 cups milk

In a saucepan, melt the butter and the molasses together, then let cool slightly. Sift all dry ingredients in a mixing bowl. Make a well in the center and scrape the butter, molasses mixture into the well. Add the eggs to the well. Begin mixing, starting from the center and mix until all the flour is incorporated. Scrape batter into a greased 9x9 inch pan. Bake at 350° for 30-40 minutes or until a toothpick inserted into the center of the cake comes out clean.

Georgia Peach Nut Bread

This is the southern fruit everyone loves. Georgia is known for it's peaches. In fact, my wife Darlene was born in Georgia, and she is quite the peach. In Alabama we get great peaches from Chilton county. Slice two slices of this bread and sandwich together with cream cheese. Very delicious!

2 cups diced Georgia peaches (fresh or frozen, drained)

1 stick butter (melted)

2/3 cup dark brown sugar

½ cup honey

1 teaspoon vanilla

1 teaspoon orange zest (optional)

¾ cup fresh orange juice

¾ cup hot coffee

2 cups flour

1 teaspoon baking soda

1 teaspoon salt

1 egg

1 cup pecan pieces

Mix all by hand. Bake at 325° for 1 hour in 2 parchment lined 9x5x3 loaf pans.

Pizza

Pecan Onion Bread

Different, yet easy, this recipe will produce 2 great loaves for you to enjoy or giveaway. The toast made from this bread is fabulous. By allowing the dough to sit overnight gives the bread an intense onion perfume.

2 cups bread flour

1 Tablespoon salt

2 Tablespoons sugar

2 packages yeast

2 cups warm milk

½ cup pecan oil or (walnut oil)

1 stick melted butter

½ cup chopped pecans

1 cup chopped onion

Mix all ingredients in mixer with dough hook until dough develops. Scrape dough into an oiled bowl and cover with plastic wrap and refrigerate over night. Punch dough down and shape into 2 equal size loaves. Place in 2 buttered 9x5x3 loaf pans. Allow to rise in a warm place until double in bulk. Bake at 400° for 40-45 minutes.

Pizza

When I was an apprentice chef in 1986, the first book my wife Darlene bought for me was titled **New American Classics** by Jeremiah Tower. I still refer to this book today. It is my hope to one day meet the Master Tower. I began making sandwiches on free form loafs of bread because of him. To this day I make all of my breads for the sandwiches at my restaurants. His pizza dough inspired me to make the best pizza I could make. To this day I make pizzas at my restaurants, but cook them over a wood fire on a grill. Wow what a great pizza. The first business I ever owned was VanIngan's Bakery and Gourmet Pizza. A friend from New York, John Krusinski, a critic of the best pizzas, helped me develop the best pizza dough recipe I have ever tasted.

3 cups bread flour

1 Tablespoon kosher salt

1 package of yeast

1 Tablespoon sugar

3 Tablespoons olive oil

1 ½ cups water

1 tomato sliced paper thin

12 Kalmata olives (pitted)

6 basil leaves

½ cup mozzarella cheese

¼ cup provolone Cheese

¼ cup parmesan cheese

In a large bowl mix the flour and salt. Make a well in the center, add yeast, sugar, olive oil and water. Mix and knead until smooth elastic dough is achieved. Lightly oil and wrap in plastic wrap and refrigerate 5-6 hours. Press out with a little flour. Stretch into a 10 inch round and sprinkle back of sheet pan with cornmeal, lay pizza dough on cornmeal. Brush dough with olive oil and lay paper thin tomatoes on top. Sprinkle chopped basil over tomatoes and distribute olives, mozzarella, provolone and Parmesan evenly over pizza. Use the cornmeal lined sheet pan like a pizza peel to slide pizza onto hot stone, or simply place pan in oven. Bake in a 500° oven on a pizza stone (preferred) for 5-7 minutes. Sprinkle with sherry vinegar and olive oil.

Actress Ashley Johnson's 16th Birthday Cake designed by Chef Bob and Cristy.

Yum!

Chapter 2
Desserts

Pecan Pie

Chapter 2

Desserts

"Sweet sister Sadie!" That's yet another southern saying. Desserts have been my passion for many years. Think about it; every time you look at an incredible dessert, you raise your eyebrows and smile from ear to ear, licking your lips in anticipation. I have never seen anyone frown at the site of something sweet, even if they had to turn it down. I can remember as a child, the first time I saw how ice cream was made. It was incredibly hot out side and Papa John (my grandfather) asked me to help him churn the ice cream. After an hour or so the churn became difficult to turn, and Papa John took over and cranked vigorously. Then, in a moment of triumph we opened the antique contraption and tasted the perfect blend of sugar, cream, vanilla, and small bits of summer peaches. The first taste was around the rim of the cylinder, with the sweet, cold ice cream and some of the rock salt brine, my tongue and palate were in total bliss. To this day it is one of my favorite memories.

" Our time left on earth is unknown, so indulge in dessert first."
Chocolate Fudge Pie

Chocolate Chip Cookies

E-Z Pie Crust

This recipe is to be used only in case of an emergency. If you can't make a good pie crust then use this no fail secret weapon.

2 cups plain flour

½ cup oil

1/3 cup milk

pinch salt

Place flour in a bowl, make a well in the center. Add oil, milk and pinch of salt. Mix into a smooth dough. Divide into 2 equal pieces. Roll out between 2 pieces of wax paper.

Pie Dough

The main thing to remember about pie dough is do not over work the dough, and let the dough rest in the refrigerator several hours before using. Pie dough freezes great!

2 ¼ cups plain flour

1 teaspoon salt

1 teaspoon sugar

¾ cup shortening (or lard)

6-7 Tablespoons ice water

Cut shortening into flour. With a fork stir in ice water and mix until dough forms. Wrap in plastic wrap and refrigerate several hours before use.

Sweet Pie Dough

This pie dough or tart dough makes a beautiful crust. If you need a pre-baked pie shell, use this recipe.

2 ½ cups of flour

¼ cup sugar

2 sticks cold butter (cut in pieces)

2 eggs

Blend together flour, sugar, and butter. Add eggs and mix until just blended.

This pie dough can be used for all pies if you like. It is fool proof.

Old Fashioned Tea Cakes

The English settlers brought with them tea time. Keeping that tradition, the heat in the Deep South forced the Southern dilatants to invent iced tea and mint juleps. You can't have tea time in the south without the famous southern tea cake. A cross between a biscuit and a sugar cookie.

6 cups plain flour

2 sticks butter

1 teaspoon baking powder

½ teaspoon baking soda

1 teaspoon lemon extract

2 cups sugar

2 eggs

½ teaspoon salt

1 teaspoon nutmeg

1/3 cup buttermilk

Sift dry ingredients into a bowl. Make a well in center and add all other ingredients. Mix with your hands into a smooth stiff dough. Chill 3-4 hours. Roll out dough on lightly floured surface about 1/2 inch thick. Cut into rounds. Bake on ungreased sheet pan at 375° for 10 minutes. Do not brown.

Southern Sweet Tea

Nothing identifies a true southerner like sweet tea (sweetened ice tea). Every restaurant server in the Deep-South will ask you, the customer "Sweet or un sweet?" In the south we know the server is asking if we would like sweetened or unsweetened iced tea. You will not see this anywhere else in the United States. It has to be because of the intense southern heat that some genius invented iced tea. There is only one way to make perfect sweet tea, my way.

4-1-quart tea bags (black and orange peeko blend)

4 cups cold water

½ cup brown sugar

1 cup white sugar

8 sprigs fresh mint

more mint for garnishing glasses

slices of lemon

Place tea bags in a 1-gallon serving container. Bring 4 cups of cold water to a boil. Turn off heat and pour hot water over tea bags. Cover container and allow to steep for 10 minutes. Remove tea bags. Do not squeeze bags too much or tea will be bitter. Add mint and sugars and stir until sugars are dissolved. Add ice water to container until 1-gallon container is full. Stir and serve over ice with a slice of lemon and a fresh sprig of mint.

Mint Julep

The Derby, a southern tradition in Kentucky that began in the late 1800's, and an excuse to sip Kentucky bourbon with lots of crushed ice (to stay cool you know). It seems to date back to at least 1885. The Kentucky Derby serves over 80,000 mint juleps during the weekend race. That's a lot of cooling off. It is said that to make a mint julep for someone is an art. This recipe makes one julep. Don't drink more than one, if you can.

1 tall slender glass

1 Tablespoon sugar

2 sprigs fresh mint

2 ounces Kentucky bourbon

3 cups crushed ice

In a lint free towel place ice and mint, fold towel and pulverize with a wooden mallet. Place sugar in bottom of glass. Pack glass tightly with minted ice. Pour bourbon over ice and serve with a long teaspoon, so you can stir occasionally to mix the sugar in. If you have to make a larger batch (not traditional) you can make a syrup with 1 cup of sugar, 1 cup of water and 4 sprigs of chopped mint. Bring to a boil and allow to cool in refrigerator over night. Fill a glass with crushed ice, pour 2 Tablespoons of minted syrup over ice, add 2 ounces of bourbon. Don't drink more than one!

Mama's Fudge

It's midnight, and you know there is some fudge in an airtight container somewhere in the house. Where did you, or the last person who had the fudge put it? It is a hunt that will end with a smile, a cold glass of milk, and a sigh. Fudge is one of those things that are so rich you have to cut into small pieces. Eating a small piece of fudge can make your sugar and chocolate cravings go away quickly, but you won't feel so guilty because the pieces are so small.

2 cups sugar

1 ½ cups heavy cream

18 ounces bitter sweet chocolate (broken into pieces)

½ cup marshmallow cream

¾ cup pecan pieces

1 stick unsalted butter

pinch salt

Bring sugar and cream to a boil in a heavy bottomed pot and cook for 10 minutes. Place all other ingredients in a medium mixing bowl. After sugar and cream have boiled for 10 minutes, pour over other ingredients and stir until chocolate and butter are melted.

Scrape the fudge into a buttered casserole dish or sheet pan. Allow to cool at room temperature until set. Cut into about 48 to 60 pieces. Store in airtight container.

Chocolate Chip Cookies

This is the one. The best chocolate chip cookie recipe in the world. It took trial and error to develop this recipe. Make this cookie dough ahead and freeze it. So, the next time you want cookies just thaw the dough, scoop and bake.

1 ½ sticks butter

1 ½ cups sugar

1 ½ cups brown sugar

1 teaspoon salt

3 extra large eggs

1 teaspoon vanilla

1 Tablespoon water

4 cups flour (sifted)

1 teaspoon baking soda

2 cups pecan pieces

24 ounces semi-sweet chocolate chips

Cream butter, sugars, and salt, add eggs slowly, add vanilla and water. Sift the flour and soda and add to batter. Fold in pecans and chocolate. Drop by a Tablespoon full on a non-stick cookie sheet and bake at 350° 12-13 minutes. Do not over cook. The cookies will continue to bake on the hot pan for a couple of minutes.

Brownies

When I was at the Waldorf-Astoria in New York, I learned this very moist brownie from the pastry chef at Peacock Alley restaurant. Don't over bake. The heat from the pan should carry over enough to finish any questionable doneness. A warm brownie, a scoop of chocolate ice cream and some chocolate sauce, should satisfy any uncontrollable chocolate urges.

1 ½ sticks unsalted butter

6 ounces bitter sweet chocolate (chopped)

1 cup dark brown sugar

1 cup sugar

1 1/3 cup flour

1 teaspoon salt

2 teaspoons baking powder

1 ½ teaspoon vanilla

4 eggs

½ cup of pecan pieces

Melt butter and chocolate in a heavy bottom pot. Remove from heat. Sift in sugars, flour, salt, and baking powder. Add to chocolate and butter mixture. Add eggs, one at a time, add vanilla and pecan pieces. Grease a 9x13 sheet pan and scrape batter into pan. Bake at 325° for 20 to 25 minutes.

Deep South Sweet Potato Pie

So very common 200 years ago and now people who taste a sweet potato pie for the first time can't wait until the next time, and the next time, and the next time and…, you get the idea. This is probably the easiest recipe for pie I have ever used. I like it warm, with ice-cold milk.

3 sweet potatoes

1 stick butter

1 cup sugar

2 eggs

1 pinch nutmeg

2 teaspoons vanilla

1-9 inch unbaked pie shell

Wash, dry, and lightly oil sweet potatoes. Bake at 350° for 45-50 minutes. While potatoes are still hot, peel and place in a hand bowl. Add all ingredients and mix until combined and butter is melted. Scrape into a 9 inch pie shell and bake at 350° for 35-40 minutes. This is a recipe developed from the 1800's.

Pecan Pie

Pecans are the nuts of the south. The trees are everywhere, providing shade, food for squirrels, excellent smoking wood, furniture and great desserts for you and me. The big secret in this recipe is the salt. It takes the intense sugar and syrup down to a level that the tongue will enjoy. Do not over bake. Wrap with plastic wrap and refrigerate or freeze.

1 cup sugar

1 teaspoon salt

3 eggs

½ stick butter (melted)

2 cups light corn syrup

1 Tablespoon vanilla

1 cup (heaping) pecan pieces

1-9 inch unbaked pie shell

Mix all ingredients together in order, except pecans, by hand with a wire whisk. Place heaping cup of pecan pieces in pie shell. Pour pie filling over pecans. Bake at 350° 35-40 minutes. For a tastier twist, sauté nuts in the butter for 2-3 minutes then flame' with the vanilla. Add the sautéed pecans to the pie shell and proceeded with recipe.

Sweet Potato Pecan pie

Why not combine two great pies. This one is fun because everyone thinks it is a pecan pie. Surprise, surprise, surprise!

½ recipe sweet potato pie

¾ cup sugar

¾ cup corn syrup

1 egg

1 Tablespoon melted butter

1 teaspoon vanilla

½ teaspoon salt

¾ cup pecan pieces

1-10 inch unbaked pie shell

Spread 1/2 recipe sweet potato pie in bottom of a 10 inch pie shell. Mix all other ingredients in a hand bowl. Pour on top of sweet potato pie mixture. Bake for 30-40 minutes at 350°. Serve with ice cream.

Apple Pie

Apple trees grow well in the Deep South. This recipe is very old and very good. I am not a fan of big apple wedges in my apple pie. It is difficult to get a good slice to stay intact. I prefer to use large wedges in cobblers. In this recipe I ask you to grate the apples on a box grater, this is the perfect apple pie, enjoy!!!! Make some cinnamon **ice cream (see index)** to go with this pie. It would almost be a crime not to.

5-6 granny smith apples

5 Tablespoons fresh lemon juice

¼ teaspoon salt

¼ teaspoon cinnamon

2 Tablespoons cornstarch

4 cups sugar

2 unbaked pie crusts

Glaze:

½ stick butter

½ cup brown sugar

1/8 teaspoon salt

Roll out bottom crust into a 9 inch pie plate. Peel, then using a grater on the largest openings, grate apples into a bowl. Mix lemon juice with apples. Mix dry ingredients and toss with apples. Scrape into pie shell. Roll out another pie shell and place on top of apple mixture. Bake pie for 30-35 minutes at 350°. Melt glaze ingredients and brush over hot pie, then bake an additional 8-10 minutes at the same 350°. Try a piece of this pie with a slice of white cheddar cheese melted over the top.

Lemon Buttermilk Chess Pie

In the 1800's American homes had a wooden chest to put pies in to keep flies and people away. It was a recipe that didn't need to stay cold. I can only assume that this is how the chess (chest) pie got it's name.

2 eggs

1 cup sugar

1 Tablespoon flour

1 Tablespoon corn meal

1 cup Buttermilk

¼ stick butter melted

¼ cup lemon juice

1-9inch pie dough

Mix all ingredients in a medium bowl with a whisk. Pour into pie shell and bake at 350° 40-50 minutes.

Chocolate Fudge Pie

This recipe my friends, is a winner. Once you make this pie it will be a favorite of yours. When the pie is done it will be slightly puffy with a gelatin mold-like shake. Let the pie cool at room temperature for at least 1 hour before cutting, if you can.

2 sticks butter

1 cup bittersweet chocolate

¾ cup dark brown sugar

1 cup white sugar

2 Tablespoons flour

4 eggs

4 Tablespoons heavy cream

2 teaspoons vanilla

1-9inch pie crust (unbaked)

Melt butter and chocolate together. Mix all ingredients together. Pour into pie shell.

Bake in 325° oven for 45-55 minutes. Ice-cold milk in a glass and a piece of this pie still warm, creates a pleasure that is indescribable.

Caramel Pie

I love this recipe for the ease of preparation and the satisfying results. Take caution not to burn the sugar. Melt the sugar with the butter until it begins to boil. This should only take a few minutes. Allow to cool 3-5 minutes and proceed with recipe. This pie is only good for 1 to 2 days, but I don't think you will have to worry about any leftovers.

1 cup brown sugar

4 Tablespoons butter

3 Tablespoons cornstarch

1 cup milk

1 egg

1 egg yolk

1 teaspoon vanilla

1 baked 9 inch pie shell

Melt butter and brown sugar in a non-stick pan. Mix milk, corn starch, add egg and egg yolk. Add melted sugar and butter. Cook over a double boiler until thickened (about 8-10 minutes). Pour into baked pie shell and allow to cool. Top with **perfect meringue (see index)**. Try brown sugar in meringue instead of white sugar. Brown in hot oven at 400° or use a blow- torch.

Vinegar pie

This interesting pie was invented in the 1800's because of lack of anything to make a pie. It became more popular during The Depression even though sugar was an expensive commodity.

2 eggs

5 Tablespoons apple cider vinegar

2 teaspoons fresh lemon juice

8 Tablespoons flour

2 cups sugar

1 ¾ cup boiling water

1 baked pie shell

Combine sugar and flour. In a heavy bottomed saucepan bring water to a boil, add sugar and flour mixture and cook for about 5 minutes. Add eggs and stir in vinegar and lemon juice, cook for 2-3 minutes. Spread into a baked pie shell. Serve.

Green Tomato Pie

A very strange, but delicious pie. Made like an apple pie, the tomatoes are tart, firm and hold their shape well. Don't tell anyone what kind of pie it is until they have had a slice. Let them guess. I developed this recipe from an idea of early French tomato conserve. A kind of tomato jam.

3 or 4 green tomatoes sliced thin (tomatoes must be hard and green)

4 cups sugar

1 teaspoon salt

¼ teaspoon cinnamon

2 Tablespoons corn starch

8 Tablespoons lemon juice

1 Tablespoon lemon zest (optional)

2-9 inch unbaked pie shells

Mix dry ingredients in a large bowl. Toss green tomatoes with dry ingredients. Add lemon juice and zest. Scrape mixture into a 9 inch pie shell. Top with lattice or another pie shell. Bake at 350° for 35-40 minutes.

Shaker Lemon Pie

A dear friend gave me this recipe. Her great grand parents were shakers. The Shakers were a group of settlers in 1770 that would have church services and shake and tremble to rebuke evil from their bodies. Known at first as the Shaker Quakers, the Shakers are credited for many inventions of pure and simple products, but perfect. If you are a lemon fan you will love this pie.

4 lemons

4 extra large eggs

2 ½ cups sugar

½ teaspoon salt

2 pie crusts

Use a V-slicer or a very sharp knife and slice lemons paper thin, rind and all. Try to pick some of the seeds out. Mix lemons with sugar and salt, let stand overnight. The next morning, beat eggs and mix with lemon mixture. Scrape into a 9 inch pie crust and top with another pie crust. Make a couple of slits in the top of the crust. Bake at 450° for12-15 minutes. Reduce heat to 375° and bake for 20 minutes, or until a knife inserted in the center comes out clean. Cool to room temperature before serving.

Butter Pound Cake

A good friend and eccentric southern lady gave me this recipe and is at least 100 years old, the recipe, not Miss Emily.

1 pound powdered sugar

3 sticks soft butter

6 eggs add slowly (2 at a time)

4 cups cake flour

2 teaspoons vanilla extract

Mix butter and powdered sugar, add eggs slowly, scrape down. Sift cake flour and add. Add vanilla flavor. Butter pan. Sprinkle with almonds if desired. Scrape batter into a loaf pan. Sprinkle top of batter with almonds if desired. Bake at 300° 1 hour 15 min. Thanks to our Emily.

Hot Water Chocolate Cake

Hot Water Chocolate Cake

A quick and easy chocolate cake that will never fail you. You don't need a mixer, you can make this with a stiff whisk and a mixing bowl. Use a mixer for ease and speed.

1 ½ cups plain flour

1 ½ cups sugar

1 teaspoon salt

1 teaspoon baking soda

1 ½ teaspoons baking powder

5 Tablespoons cocoa powder

1 stick butter

1 ½ cups hot (boiling) water

1 egg

2 teaspoons vanilla

Sift first 6 ingredients into a mixer bowl fitted with the paddle attachment. Add 1 stick of soft butter. Bring water to a boil. Turn mixer on low speed, and begin to add the boiling water. Add egg and vanilla and beat on medium speed for about 3 minutes. Pour into greased and dusted with cocoa powder, two 8 inch or two 9 inch pans. Bake at 340° for 20-25 minutes. Ice with **old fashioned chocolate icing (see index).**

Carrot Cake

Who came up with putting carrots in a cake? I don't know, but I do know that this recipe will make you blissful. It's easy and very moist. Peel, then grate the carrots on a box grater.

The carrots loose something when you grind them in a food processor.

1 ½ cups canola oil

3 cups sugar

4 eggs

2 cups grated carrots

2 teaspoons vanilla

2 cups flour

2 teaspoons baking powder

1 ½ teaspoons baking soda

1 teaspoon salt

2 teaspoons cinnamon

1-12ounce can crushed pineapple (drained)

½ cup pecan pieces

Mix first five ingredients in a mixer for 5 minutes on medium speed. Sift flour, baking powder, baking soda, salt, and cinnamon.

Add to mixer. Add drained, crushed pineapple and pecans. Mix for 3 minutes on medium speed. Grease two nine-inch cake pans and line with a buttered parchment paper circle. Divide batter equally between pans and bake at 350° for 45-50 minutes. Cool for 10 minutes, then run a knife around cake to loosen from sides of pan. Turn out on wire racks. Allow to cool at least two hours. Frost with **cream cheese icing (see index)**.

Carrot Cake

Red Velvet Cake

Red Velvet Cake is proudly claimed as the official Christmas cake of the Deep-South. Unfortunately for the Deep-South, the recipe was a concoction, created by the pastry chef at the Waldorf-Astoria at Oscar's restaurant in the 1940's for a special guest for Christmas. The original was thought to be colored with beat juice. The Deep-South got hold of this recipe and commercialized it. In the 1970's red food dye Number 2 was banned, when it was thought to be linked to cancer, so the cake was not as popular. Now in the Deep-South the red velvet cake is almost an everyday cake and really popular as a wedding cake. Imagine that silky, moist, fire red cake hidden under a perfectly decorated, white, wedding cake icing. In the Deep-South, everyone will tell you that they have the best red velvet cake recipe, ever. Now you have the power to make that claim.

My grandmother has been famous in our family for generations, making this cake for holidays and birthday cakes. She is 85 now and not baking as much as she used to, so you the reader of this book and myself will have to carry the red velvet torch from this day forward, into the world of the red velvet cake challenged.

1 ½ cups sugar

1 ½ cups canola oil

3 eggs

2 ½ cups cake flour (sifted twice)

1 teaspoon baking soda

1 teaspoon salt

½ teaspoon baking powder

1 cup buttermilk

2 Tablespoons cocoa

1 teaspoon red wine vinegar

2 ounce bottle red food color

2 teaspoons vanilla

Using a mixer, with whip attachment, mix oil, eggs, and sugar on medium speed until creamy and thickened. Sift flour, baking soda, salt, and baking powder in a separate bowl twice. Mix cocoa, vinegar, and food color in a small cup or bowl. Add to egg and oil mixture. Alternate dry ingredients with buttermilk into the mixer. Mix on medium speed for 2-3 minutes until you achieve a smooth cake batter. Pour into three, 8-inch greased cake pans. Bake at 350° for 25-35 minutes, or until a wooden toothpick inserted into the middle of the cake comes out clean. Let cakes rest 5 minutes and then turn out on wire racks and cool completely. Frost with **cream cheese** icing. Decorate with crushed pecans and a few red velvet cake crumbs.

Cheese Cake

Invest in a restaurant quality spring form pan. The results are worth it. You can keep this cake covered in the refrigerator for 2-3 days or it freezes great. You can flavor this batter by adding peanut butter and bananas or chocolate **ganache**, or orange marmalade or use your imagination.

<u>Crust</u>

1 ½ cups graham cracker crumbs

1 stick unsalted butter (melted)

½ cup sugar

Mix together and press into 9 inch spring form pan. Bake for 10 minutes at 350°.

<u>Cake</u>

2-8 ounce packages cream cheese

1 cup sugar

1 stick butter, softened

5 eggs

2 cups sour cream

1 Tablespoon vanilla

In a mixer with the paddle attachment, mix the cream cheese, butter, and sugar until smooth. Scrape down bowl and paddle with a rubber scraper. Add eggs slowly. Scrape bowl and paddle again. Add sour cream and vanilla. Scrape into the graham crust. Bake in a water bath in a 350° oven for 2 hours. After first hour loosely cover with foil and continue baking the second hour. Allow to cool over night in refrigerator. Run a knife around cake edge of the cake before unlocking pan latch.

Japanese Fruit Cake

This is a recipe that my wife's grandmother used to make. It is a strange, yet delicious cake. Do not use cake flour or this cake will fall apart. I know from experience

2 cups sugar

3 sticks butter

6 eggs (separated)

4 cups flour

2 teaspoons baking powder

1 teaspoon allspice

½ teaspoon cinnamon

½ teaspoon nutmeg

½ teaspoon ground cloves

1 cup milk

1 cup of soaked raisins (soaked in brandy)

In a mixer bowl with paddle attachment, mix butter and sugar until light and creamy. Add egg yolks and mix for 2-3 minutes. Scrape down bowl and paddle. Sift dry ingredients. Alternate wet and dry ingredients. Whip egg whites until semi stiff peaks. Fold egg whites into batter. Divide into three 8-inch paper lined cake pans. Bake at 325° 20-30 minutes.

Frosting

Juice and rind of 2 lemons

2 cups of sugar

1 cup of boiling water

1-12 ounce can crushed pineapple

1 can cocoa Lopez (cream of coconut)

4 Tablespoons cornstarch

Mix all ingredients and cook until thickened and spread over layers and garnish with candied ginger and cherries.

Chocolate Roulade

Years ago I use to make this cake for several restaurants. At one point I was making 50-60 every week. In other words, I have made this a few times. Don't cry if you mess up the first time or two, I did. Don't panic, just start over. Willingness and effort will make you bake like a professional.

6 eggs (separated)

½ cup sugar

4 Tablespoons sugar (for the egg whites)

6 ounces bitter-sweet chocolate

¼ cup boiling coffee

1 stick melted butter

Filling

2 cups of heavy cream

½ cup of powdered sugar

1 teaspoons vanilla

Bring coffee to a boil and pour over chocolate. Mix until smooth. In a mixer with the whip attachment, place the egg yolks and 1/2 cup of sugar. Whip until yolks are thick and light yellow in color. Transfer this mixture into a medium mixing bowl. Clean mixer bowl and whip attachment. Fold chocolate mixture into egg yolk mixture. In a clean mixer whip egg whites to soft moist peeks.

Add the 4 Tablespoons of sugar to the whites while whipping. Line a half sheet pan with parchment paper and paint with melted butter. Fold whites into the chocolate egg yolk mixture. Scrape into prepared pan and slide into a 350° oven for 18-20 minutes. Allow to cool for 1 hour. Whip the 2 cups of heavy cream until stiff peaks form. Fold in the powdered sugar and vanilla. Loosen cake by running a knife around the pan edges, turn out onto a parchment paper. If the cake is a little sticky, dust parchment with cocoa powder. Spread whipped cream over cake and roll cake up like a jelly roll or a delicate, expensive rug using the parchment to help the rolling. Transfer to a pan and place in refrigerator or freezer.

Chocolate Roulage

Old Fashioned Chocolate Icing

This is an easier version of a grandma style cooked icing. The difficult one produces almost the same result. Please, use real butter and whole milk, the dairy farmers depend on it, and the richness and smoothness of your finished icing depends on it.

1 cup cocoa (sifted)

4 sticks butter

1 pound powdered sugar

1 teaspoon vanilla

¾ cup milk

Melt butter and cocoa together. Pour over powdered sugar. Add vanilla and milk. Stir together. Beat until smooth and creamy. Beat in a mixer for 3-5 minutes.

Cream Cheese Icing

A classic icing that is guaranteed to make your cake very content. What cake would not want this sweet, smooth, creamy mixture spread all over it? Use this icing for **carrot cake, red velvet cake, chocolate cake, brownies (see index)** or whatever you have a craving for.

1-8 ounce package cream cheese (soft)

1 stick unsalted butter

1 pinch salt

1 pound 10x powdered sugar

2 teaspoons vanilla

In a mixer with the paddle attachment add the cream cheese, butter and salt. Cream until smooth. Add powdered sugar and vanilla. Beat 3-5 minutes on medium speed. Store in air tight container. Use at room temperature, then refrigerate.

Ice Cream

One of my favorite childhood memories was making ice cream with my grandfather, Papa John. It was always extremely hot outside when he decided to make ice cream. He told me to crank the handle of a very old, manual ice cream maker. As he filled the wooden bucket with ice and rock salt, steam rose from the frozen ice because of the intense summer heat. I knew that inside the old creaky bucket was something wonderful.

When the crank handle was hard to turn Papa John took over and in a couple of minutes of vigorous cranking was our moment of triumph. He lifted the lid and we took our first taste of the frozen concoction with a perfect blend of sugar, cream, vanilla, and small bits of summer peaches. The first taste was around the rim of the cylinder, with the sweet, cold ice cream and some of the rock salt brine, my tongue and palate were in total bliss, taking me to ice cream glory, bite after bite.

1 quart half and half

2 cups heavy cream

1 cup sugar

10 egg yolks

1 cup sugar

1 vanilla bean (split and seeds scraped into cream)

In a heavy bottomed pot bring half and half, 1 cup of sugar, cream, vanilla bean and seeds to a boil. In a medium mixing bowl mix egg yolks and sugar. Temper egg yolk mixture by slowly whisking hot liquid to egg yolk mixture. Whisk egg mixture back into pot and cook stirring but <u>do not </u>bring back to a boil. Make a track with your finger on the back of a spoon dipped into the hot liquid. If the track does not disappear, it's done! Strain through a fine sieve into a bowl. Set the bowl in a larger bowl filled with ice. Whisk occasionally until cold. Remove vanilla bean. Freeze custard in a home ice cream freezer according to manufacturer's instructions. When ice cream is almost finished you can add fresh peaches, blueberries or what ever you like, then finish freezing.

Ice Cream

Caramelized Pecans

This is a little tricky because the nuts can burn quickly. Just keep them moving in the pan. You can give these nuts as gifts in a decorative glass jar.

2 cups sugar

1 cup water

1 teaspoon salt

3 ½ cups pecan halves

Bring sugar and water to a boil in a heavy bottomed pot. Add pecans. Let cook, stirring occasionally until large bubbles disappear and nuts become dry and sandy. Now stir often while the sandy sugar begins to melt. The nuts will burn in just a few seconds if you are not careful. When most of the sandy sugar is melted and somewhat golden brown, remove from heat and spread out on a silpat (non stick mat) or parchment paper. After the nuts cool, break apart and keep in an air tight container for weeks, if you can keep your hands off of them.

Banana Pudding

My grandmother made banana pudding, it seemed like every weekend. She would spend about an hour or so just slicing and layering. Vanilla cookie, banana slice, vanilla cookie, banana slice, vanilla cookie, banana slice. Every banana slice was the exact same size and next to a corresponding cookie. I have taken a different approach, by slicing all of the bananas and adding the box of vanilla cookies, then stirring to combine somewhat evenly. I also like using milk instead of sweetened condensed milk. This recipe can double as a pie filling: Banana cream pie, coconut cream, or even chocolate cream. Be sure to stir continuously so as not to scorch the pudding. If it scorches, throw it out and start over.

3 cups milk

1 cup sugar

Bring milk and 1 cup of sugar to a boil.

1 cup sugar

3 Tablespoons cornstarch

4 eggs

2 egg yolks

1 stick butter

3 teaspoons vanilla

1 box of vanilla wafers (cookies)

1 bunch of bananas

Introduce slowly, the boiling milk and sugar to the egg, sugar, and cornstarch mixture. Pour back into the pot you boiled the milk in and cook until thick and bubbly. Stir constantly. Be careful, the mixture is very hot, take off heat and whisk in the butter and vanilla. Begin slicing bananas in a decorative bowl of your choice, and add 1 box of vanilla wafers. Stir to mix the cookies and bananas, to a somewhat, even distribution. Pour hot filling over cookies and bananas. Shake bowl gently to allow filling to seep into bowl. Top with perfect meringue. Brown in 425° oven for 5 minutes or use a blowtorch.

Chocolate Cobbler

4 cups milk

1 cup sugar

Bring milk and sugar to a boil.

1 cup sugar

3 Tablespoons cornstarch

4 eggs

2 egg yolks

1 stick butter

3 teaspoons vanilla

1 cup of bitter-sweet chocolate (chopped)

Introduce slowly, the boiling milk and sugar to the egg, sugar, and cornstarch mixture. Pour back into the pot you boiled the milk in and cook until thick and bubbly. Stir constantly. Be careful the mixture is very hot, take off heat and whisk in the butter and vanilla, add the chopped chocolate. Scrape the filling into a decorative dish. Top with a baked piece of puff pastry, cut to fit the decorative dish. Top with powdered sugar.

Peach Cobbler

Peaches are as common as grits in the Deep-South. Peach **ice cream**, peach fried pies, **brandied peaches (see index)**, peach jam, and peach cobbler are the most common uses.

8 peaches (fresh preferred)

1 cup peach juice (from brandied peaches, yum)

1 cup sugar

1 ½ Tablespoons cornstarch

pinch of salt

pinch of cinnamon

Peel and slice peaches. Mix all other ingredients in a saucepan and bring to a boil. Take off heat and add peaches. Pour into a casserole and top with **Mattie's biscuit (see index)** dough. Roll out dough and lay on top of peach filling. I like to lay a thin layer on bottom and then cut dough into strips and make a lattice pattern. Sprinkle with sugar and bake for 30-40 minutes at 350°.

Perfect Meringue

The title is the truth. This is perfect meringue. Separate eggs while they are cold and whip them when they are room temperature. Make sure the mixer bowl and whip attachment is very clean and dry.

4 egg whites

3 teaspoons cornstarch

3 Tablespoons sugar

By hand or in a mixer with a whip attachment, whip egg whites until very foamy. Mix cornstarch and sugar together, sprinkle into egg whites. Beat until stiff, moist peeks develop. This will take about 5 to 10 minutes.

Southern Divinity

For over 200 years this candy has been a tradition in the south, and high society southern ladies would judge each other on how their divinity tasted and looked. You need a good candy thermometer and no rain. Too much humidity will make this candy sticky.

½ cup corn syrup (light corn syrup)

2 ½ cups sugar

¼ teaspoon salt

½ cup water

2 egg whites

1 teaspoon vanilla

1 cup chopped pecans

Mix water, sugar, syrup and salt in a heavy bottomed saucepan. Cook stirring until sugar dissolves. Continue cooking without stirring until a candy thermometer reaches 248°. Beat egg whites while sugar is cooking. Beat until stiff, moist peaks. While mixer is running pour half of the syrup slowly into the egg whites. Leave machine running on slow speed. Cook remaining syrup to 272° and slowly add into egg white mixture. Beat on medium high until mixture holds its shape. Fold in vanilla and nuts. Drop by Tablespoon full on wax paper. My wife's grandmother was famous for this old recipe.

Southern Pecan Brittle

Peanut and pecan brittle are very popular candy in the Deep-South. It can be compared in popularity to Louisiana's pralines. Almost every store and gas station in the south has bricks of this crunchy, addicting candy. Every Christmas stocking in the Deep-South should have some brittle in them. This recipe will work better on low humidity days. In other words, don't make this when it's raining outside, the candy will turn out a little sticky.

1 ½ cups sugar

¾ cup clear corn syrup

1 ½ Tablespoon water

1 ½ teaspoon baking soda

3 cups pecan halves

Mix the sugar, corn syrup, and water in a heavy bottomed pot. Cook on high heat for 6 minutes and add pecans. Continue to cook for 10-12 minutes, until sugar begins to caramelize (turn light brown). Take away from stove and stir in the baking soda. Don't be startled, the mixture will foam up. Continue to mix for 1 minute. Scrape onto a greased cookie sheet. After cooled, break into pieces and wrap in plastic wrap. Eat some and give the rest away. If you don't give it away you will eat it all.

Chocolate Oatmeal Cookies

Chocolate drop cookies, no bake cookies, boiled cookies, cow patties. It has a lot of names, but has only one taste, good. My friend Robbie turned me on to this recipe. I developed it for commercial use and made thousands. Without exaggerating too much, he and I have made over 500,000 of these babies.

1 cup milk

1 cup shortening

8 Tablespoons cocoa (heaping)

4 cups sugar

1 cup peanut butter

2 teaspoons vanilla

1 pound Quick oats

Bring the first four ingredients to a boil for 2-3 minutes. (stirring occasionally). Add peanut butter & vanilla, stir and add oats quickly. Drop from scoop on wax paper. When cookies are set, store in air tight containers.

Chef Bob & Claude Troigros

Chapter 3
Deep-South Vegetables

Sir Robert "Chef Bob" Vaningan O.S.C.

Chapter 3

Deep-South Vegetables

"Got any good vegetables?" and, "It aint fittin, not to have good vegetables. "These are words you hear often in the Deep-South. Vegetables grow very happily in the summer months and entire meals sometimes consist of "good vegetables". Back in the 1700's the big deep-south crop was rice. Corn, introduced by Native American Indians was cultivated and refined into everything. Did you know that a lot of snack foods in the Deep-South are made from grits? What is a grit? Grits are made of corn. The white corn is dried and ground under a stone, leaving a small amount of bran. After cooking the grits, the gritty texture remains, hence the name grits.

Hominy is yellow corn that has been soaked in lye water to remove the bran, the corn swells to at least double in size. The hominy is dried again and ground into hominy grits. A lot of what's called Deep South cuisine has been transplanted. Africa is where Turnips, collards, black-eyed peas, watermelon and okra came from. These are some of the vegetables that define Deep South cooking and bring us together with real soul food.

What is soul food? Simply food that is cooked with so much love and respect, for the food and the people you are cooking for, it comes from the soul.

Fried Green Tomatoes

A concoction so famous they made a whole movie out of it. Watch the movie or read the book when you make this recipe, and you will get a small feeling of being here in my world, The Deep South.

3 green tomatoes

½ cup plain flour

½ teaspoon salt and pepper

1 cup buttermilk

1 egg

1 teaspoon salt

1 teaspoon pepper

1 cup cracker meal

2 cups oil

Make sure the tomatoes are hard. Slice the green tomatoes in 1/2 inch slices. Mix salt and pepper in the 1/2 cup of flour. Mix the buttermilk and egg in a separate bowl. Mix salt and pepper into the cracker meal in yet another bowl. Heat oil to 350° for frying. Dredge the tomato slices in the seasoned flour. Dip into the buttermilk and egg. Dip into the seasoned cracker meal. Fry in hot oil for 3 minutes or until golden brown. Remove tomatoes from oil and drain on paper towels. Sprinkle a little salt and pepper on the hot tomatoes.

Turnip Greens

Turnip greens, collards, and mustard greens, a Deep-South staple. In my travels to New York and some very fine dining establishments I found baby turnips with sautéed baby turnip greens. How very gourmet and how very southern!

3 large bunches fresh turnip greens

2 split ham hocks (smoked)

1 Tablespoon kosher salt

1 Tablespoon black pepper

2 Tablespoons sugar

3 Tablespoons cider vinegar

2-3 quarts water

In a large pot, bring water, hocks, salt, pepper, sugar, and vinegar, to a boil. Cook hocks for about 45 minutes to 1 hour. Strip leaves off turnip stems and place leaves in large container or sink, full of cold water. Plunge hands in and out of sink full of greens for 2-3 minutes. Change water and repeat this process 3 times. Drain the water from sink and begin adding greens to boiling ham hock water, stirring leaves down as they wilt. Turn heat down to simmering and cook until tender, about 1 hour. Serve with **corn pones**, or **corn bread (see index)**, and black-eyed peas or pinto beans. Don't forget the slice of raw onion, very traditional southern combination.

Black-eyed Peas

Black-eyed peas are one of those vegetables that came from Africa. In the Deep South on New Year's day, eat a big bowl of black-eyes for prosperity and collard greens for hopes of lots of folding money, one must. I wonder if the black-eyed pea and collard green farmer came up with that tradition? Enjoy these peas with their favorite companion, turnip greens or collard greens. In the Deep South, a bowl with turnip greens and black-eyed peas are called a half & half. Appropriate corn bread and slice of onion must be accompanied.

1 onion (chopped)

3 cloves garlic (chopped)

3 ounces salt pork (optional)

1 sprig fresh thyme (1/2 teaspoon dried thyme)

1 Tablespoon sugar

1 Tablespoon vinegar

2 teaspoons salt

1 teaspoon black pepper

1 pound black-eyed peas (washed)

Black-eyed peas are found fresh in the Deep South all summer long. Then we find frozen or lastly, dried. All forms are good but dried beans need care. Usually you will find a rock or two and some dirt. Just wash and pick through them. Let them soak for 2 hours in hot water, drain and rinse in cold water and you are ready to cook.

Dice salt pork and sauté in a heavy bottomed pot. If you choose not to use the salt pork (I can't imagine that), sauté onion and garlic in 3 Tablespoons of olive oil until soft but <u>not</u> caramelized. If you use the salt pork (yeah!) after it has rendered some fat, add the onion and garlic and cook until soft. Add all other ingredients and cover peas generously with cold water and bring to a boil, reduce to a simmer and cook until tender, about 45 minutes to 1 hour.

Collard Greens

Pinto Beans

1 onion diced

3 Tablespoons oil

1 smoked ham hock

2 sprigs fresh thyme (1 teaspoon dried thyme)

1 pound dried pinto beans

Wash and pick through beans, soak over night in a generous amount of cold water. Drain and rinse beans. Sauté onions in oil until soft. Add ham hock and brown. Add thyme. Add beans and cover with a generous amount of water, bring to a boil, reduce heat to a simmer. Cook until tender, about 1 to 1 1/2 hours. Add salt and pepper. Pintos are a meal all by them selves, with a slice of Vidalia onion and a piece of **cornbread (see index)**. Humble, but so satisfying.

Fried Okra

Okra is an African vegetable (Kumba) that found its way to America in the early 1600's. If you can find baby okra, fry the whole pod. You will never seem to have enough fried okra. I can eat fried okra like a big bowl of popcorn.

1 pound fresh young okra

4 cups plain flour

3 teaspoons salt

2 teaspoons black pepper

1 cup plain corn meal

3 cups buttermilk

2 eggs

4 cups vegetable oil (peanut oil preferred)

Heat oil to 345° in a deep, heavy-bottomed pot. In a medium mixing bowl, mix salt, pepper and flour. Divide flour mixture into 2 mixing bowls. Add the corn meal to the second bowl of flour. In yet another medium mixing bowl, whisk eggs and buttermilk. Wash okra and then slice in 1/2 inch slices. Toss 1/3 of the sliced okra in the flour, then in the egg mixture, then in the second flour mixture, coating well. Fry until golden brown. Remove with a slotted spoon from fryer and drain on paper towels or paper sacks. Sprinkle with salt if needed. Repeat until all okra is used.

Rutabagas

This is an underrated vegetable that is full of vitamins, tastes great, and is very low in cost. Thought to have come to North America in the 1600's and grow well in the Deep South, southerners have adopted the humble rutabaga as one of its southern vegetables.

2 rutabagas

4 pieces smoked bacon (cubed)

¼ cup sugar

¼ cup apple cider vinegar

Salt & Pepper

Cube bacon and sauté in a heavy bottomed pot. Peel and cube rutabagas and add to pot. Add sugar and vinegar and just enough water to cover rutabagas. Bring to a boil, simmer for 1 hour or until tender. Adjust seasoning with salt and pepper.

Sweet Potato Casserole

Sweet potatoes are as popular as corn in the Deep South. I think North Carolina and Mississippi are the largest producers. Sweet potatoes came from South America and resemble the African yam. Yams are not sweet potatoes. There have been some hybrids, but true yams are almost white and grow in Africa and Jamaica. Yams from Japan and China are very long and very sticky when cooked. Sweet potatoes are orange, shorter and fatter than yams. For some reason, maybe tradition, sweet potato casserole has to be served with ham. The flavor of ham was made to accompany sweet potatoes.

6 sweet potatoes

1 cup heavy cream

2 sticks butter

1 cup brown sugar

1 teaspoon cinnamon

½ teaspoon nutmeg

1 bag marshmallows (Big ones)

Bake sweet potatoes for 40-50 minutes. Allow to cool 30 minutes then peel. Mash all ingredients together except marshmallows. Scrape into a casserole dish, top with marshmallows and brown in 400° oven 5-10 minutes.

Sweet Potato Cress

This recipe is one I have enjoyed every Christmas for 40 years. My grandmother (Mama Payne) gave me this glorious recipe for everyone who may read this book. It is very sweet, but very good. This is one of those flavors that when you taste it, no matter what mood you are in, you will instantly smile and sigh between bites. It looks beautiful on a Christmas table in a round or oval, white baking dish.

4 sweet potatoes (baked, peeled and mashed)

1 cup sugar

1 cup milk

1 egg

1 teaspoon vanilla

½ teaspoon salt

½ cup grated coconut (fresh or canned)

½ stick butter to grease pan

Mix all ingredients and scrape into a buttered casserole dish. Bake at 350° for 25-30 minutes.

Topping

1-8 ounce can crushed pineapple with juice

1-12 ounce jar Maraschino cherries with juice

1 cup sugar

3 Tablespoons cornstarch

Cook until thickened. Pour over potato casserole. Garnish with a few pecan halves if desired.

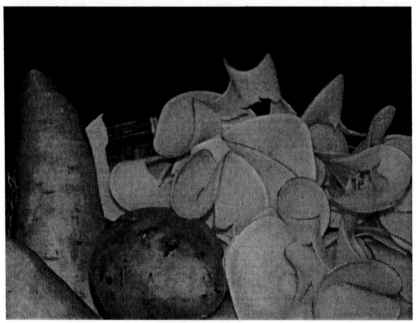

Sweet Potatoes

Tomato Aspic

Tomato aspic is a refreshing and satisfying summer salad. Aspic was very popular in the 18th and 19th century and still popular in the Deep-South. Tomato aspic can be found in older established restaurants or tearooms. Eat this in the summer with crusty French bread.

2 Tablespoons unflavored gelatin

¼ cup cold water

2 cups fresh tomato juice or V-8

¼ cup orange juice

1 small onion finely diced

1 red bell pepper finely diced

½ carrot finely diced

1 Tablespoons sugar

1 teaspoon salt

1/8 teaspoon pepper

Soften gelatin in 1/4 cup of water for 5-10 minutes. Place all other ingredients in a saucepan and bring to a boil. Turn off heat, stir in softened gelatin and pour into individual moulds. Refrigerate several hours or overnight. To present, make a bed of your favorite lettuces and dip mould into hot water for 10-15 seconds and turn out onto lettuce. Serve with crusty bread and Sherry vinaigrette.

Summer Squash Casserole

Summer squash grow like weeds in the Deep South. Squash casserole is a weekend and holiday dish we see in just about every home. I have enhanced the old south recipe with artichokes and mayo. Easy and delicious.

10 yellow summer squash

1 onion (sliced)

2 artichokes or (1 can drained)

½ cup mayonnaise

2 eggs

1 cup shredded cheddar cheese

salt and pepper

1 cup seasoned croutons (homemade preferred)

Wash and cut squash in 1/2 inch size slices. Slice onion thin as possible. Place squash and onion in a heavy bottomed pot and cover with water. Bring to a boil. Take off heat and drain in a colander. Allow squash to drain and cool about one hour. Press on squash to remove extra liquid. Mix all ingredients except croutons in a mixing bowl. Scrape mixture into a casserole dish and top with croutons. Bake 30-40 minutes at 350°

Baked Vidalia Onions

There is only one place in the world that you can get Vidalia onions, Deep South Georgia. Chefs wait all year for the harvest and have inventive tricks to prolong the shelf life of these bulbous gems. One that really works is women's panty hose. Drop an onion in the hose root first, tie a knot above the jewel. Slide another onion in, root first, and repeat this until you finish at the top. Tie at the top and hang in a basement, from a nail or hook. To use, simply cut an onion by cutting below the knot. You can also hang them in a pantry closet. I use them up so fast, I don't get to decorate with panty hose full of onions. Some people will think you have a strange sense of decorating, but they will love your onions!

6 Vidalia onions (peeled)

1 stick butter cut in 6 pieces

salt and pepper

6 sprigs fresh thyme

4 cups chicken stock

Cut an x on top of onions, place in a casserole dish. Salt and pepper onions. Place a piece of butter on top of each onion. Lay a sprig of fresh thyme on top of butter. Pour **chicken stock (see index)** in casserole dish. Wrap with aluminum foil and bake at 375° for 1 hour.

Potato and Onion Casserole

A classic French potato casserole, converted to the Deep South with Vidalia onions.

5 potatoes sliced (½ inch thick)

2 Vidalia onions

4 cups chicken stock

salt and pepper

Wash potatoes and slice into 1/2 inch slices. Blanch in boiling salted water for 3 minutes. Drain potatoes in a colander. Butter a baking dish and layer with slices of potato and then onion. Salt and pepper each layer. Pour **chicken stock (see index)** over potatoes, cover with foil and bake for 45 minutes in a 350°oven.

Green Beans

Green Beans

Traditionally in the deep-south vegetables are usually cooked far beyond any recognition of its former life as a beautiful vegetable. Young green beans are best when blanched in boiling water for 10 to 12 minutes, then shocked in an ice water bath. Any cooking beyond this point is personal preference. Use your own judgment, but please, don't cook the vegetables to death. This recipe is perfect for fresh green beans.

1 smoked ham hock

1 small onion (sliced)

3 Tablespoons oil

salt and pepper

2 pounds fresh green beans

Sauté onion in oil. Add ham hock and brown. Pour 2 quarts of water in pot and cook for 45 minutes. Clean beans and string if necessary. Add salt and pepper. Plunge beans into pot with ham hock. Reduce to a simmer and cook for 20 minutes.

Baby Lima Beans

A native bean from North America that grows well in the Deep South. Used in many recipes in the south this one is the most common.

1 ham bone (left over from baked ham)

2 sprigs fresh thyme

2 teaspoons salt

2 teaspoons sugar

2 teaspoons black pepper

2 pounds baby limas (fresh or frozen)

In a large pot place ham bone and thyme, cover with water and bring to a boil, reduce to a simmer for 1 hour. Add salt, sugar, pepper, and baby limas. Cook for 20-40 minutes until beans are tender. If you worry about flagellants, use Beano, an enzyme to alter gas production.

Butter Beans

Butter beans are grown up baby limas. Baby limas are green in color and mature limas (Butter beans) are cream color. Butter beans and corn bread are a weekly staple in the Deep South.

1 ham bone (left over from baked ham)

2 sprigs fresh thyme

1 onion diced

4 cloves garlic chopped

1 Tablespoon salt

1 Tablespoon sugar

2 teaspoons black pepper

3 Tablespoons apple cider vinegar

2 pounds Butter beans (fresh or frozen)

Place ham bone and thyme in a large pot covered with water. Bring to a boil and simmer for 1 hour. Add all other ingredients and simmer for 20-40 minutes until beans are tender. If you worry about the effect a large portion of beans will have on your body, use Beano, an enzyme to alter gas production

Creamed Corn

In the Deep South, corn is almost up there with water and air. If you have a large cast iron skillet, use it. Somehow, it seems to taste better, however, it may stick. If you use a large non-stick skillet, you won't have any problems. Don't forget to stir using a rubber spatula so you do not scratch the non-stick surface.

4 ears fresh corn (silver queen ideal)

1 Vidalia onion (chopped)

1 stick butter

salt and pepper

1 cup heavy cream

Shuck corn and cut corn off of cob, holding corn upright and cut with a sharp knife in a downward motion toward cutting board. After all corn is removed, use the back of the knife and scrape the cobs, extracting the corn juice. This is called milking the cobs. Sauté the onion in the butter until soft. Add the corn and the corn juice (milk). Add salt and pepper. Cook for 3-4 minutes. Add the heavy cream. Cook an additional 10-15 minutes, stirring occasionally. Taste for salt and pepper and add if needed. If it is too thick you can thin with milk.

If you are afraid of burning the creamed corn, bake it in a 400° oven, stirring often. This procedure takes about 45 minutes. Thanks Joyce!

Deep-South Succotash

This vegetable stew is my version of a Native American Indian classic. Thank GOD for Native Americans. The original was probably, lima beans, corn, herbs, and wild onions. You can freeze this and make a great vegetable soup by adding vegetable stock or chicken stock.

1 onion (diced)

3 green onions (chopped)

5 cloves garlic (chopped)

1 pound lima beans (fresh or frozen)

1 pound fresh corn off the cob (or frozen)

1 pound okra (sliced)

2 tomatoes (diced)

2 cups tomato juice

2 sprigs fresh thyme (1 teaspoon dried thyme)

Salt and Pepper

Sauté the onions and garlic in oil until soft. Add the other ingredients and cook for 10-15 minutes. Add salt and pepper. A sprig of an herb is a small branch with several smaller branches attached.

Grits

What are grits? Grits are stone ground white corn, a southern staple that every southern home has in their pantry. All fast food restaurants in the south make grits for their breakfast customers. I am not sure we could live without them. I beg you please, do not use instant grits. I must forbid it! I will however allow you to use quick grits, but would prefer you find stone ground white or hominy grits.

3 ½ cups water or stock

1 teaspoon salt

1 cup grits

Bring water or stock and salt to a boil. Whisk in grits, turn heat to low and cook about 20 minutes stirring occasionally. Serve with butter, salt and pepper. Use as a side dish or alone.

Fried Grits

1 recipe cooked grits

1 cup seasoned flour

1 egg beaten

½ cup buttermilk

3 cups of oil for frying

To make fried grits, pour hot grits into a loaf pan, lined with plastic wrap. Chill several hours. Turn out and slice in 1/2-inch slices.

Dip into seasoned flour, then buttermilk and egg mixture, and then back into seasoned flour. Fry in 350° oil until browned, about 2 minutes.

An alternate method is to dip into seasoned flour or seasoned corn meal and fry in butter until brown and crispy. A great side dish.

Grits Casserole

This is a perfect breakfast. Use your imagination and add what you like in this casserole.

1 recipe cooked grits

1 cup diced ham

3 eggs

1 cup heavy cream

1 cup cheddar cheese (shredded)

salt and pepper

Combine all ingredients and place in a casserole dish. Bake 30 minutes at 350°.

Macaroni and Cheese

Even though Macaroni and cheese is not a vegetable, we sure treat it like one in the Deep South. Use a deep casserole dish.

1 pound macaroni pasta

3 quarts water

4 Tablespoons salt

4 cups shredded cheese

1/2 cup parmesan cheese

1 recipe cheese sauce (see index)

Bring water and salt to a boil. Add pasta and cook for about 6-8 minutes. Drain pasta, do not rinse. Pour pasta into a large bowl, add cheese sauce, shredded cheese and parmesan cheese. Pour into a lightly buttered deep casserole dish. Top with more Parmesan and some bread crumbs if desired. Bake 35-45 minutes at 350°.

Some cooks add 3-4 eggs to this recipe. The addition of eggs will make a clean cut when serving.

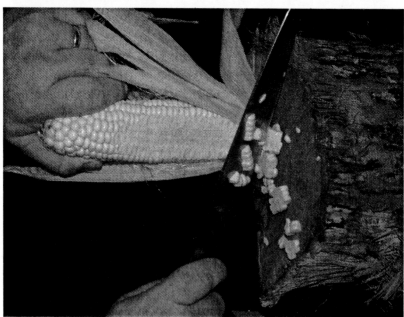

Cutting Corn for Creamed Corn

Chapter 4
Sauces & Marinades

Chapter 4
Stocks, Sauces, and Marinades

This chapter is designed to give you a home advantage of basic flavors. A good gravy needs a good stock. Once you make your own stock you will never buy stock again. Make large batches and freeze in smaller containers, pints or quarts. Label and date your stocks and try to use them up in a month or two. Always use the freshest ingredients and remember to cool stocks quickly. Have fun discovering the basics and remember, practice, practice, practice.

Stock vegetables are onion, carrot, and celery, rough cut and used to flavor the stock.

Roux

2 sticks of butter or (1 cup of oil)

1 cup plain flour

Roux pronounced (rooh) is a simple mixture of oil and flour that is cooked. You can keep roux covered in the refrigerator for weeks. Melt butter or heat oil in a wide saucepan or iron skillet. Add flour whisking quickly as to not burn the roux. Cook over medium heat stirring constantly. The more brown your roux is, the more flavor it has, but the darker the roux, the less thickening power it has. My general rule is 1/2 cup of roux should thicken 1 quart of stock. Also to avoid lumps use cold roux into a hot stock, whisking. If you still have lumps, simply strain through a sieve.

Stock Vegetables

Stock vegetables are the aromatic flavor we cooks add to our stocks. If you really want to study the art of stocks, get your hands on a copy of **The Escoffier Cookbook** by Escoffier.

1 onion

2 carrots

3 stalks of celery

For the recipes in this book simply peel vegetables and rough cut them for addition into stocks and soups. Bring whatever liquid you have chosen to a boil. Turn heat to a simmer for about 1 hour. Strain out stock vegetables and proceed with recipe. You can enhance the flavor further with the addition of herbs.

Basic Chicken Stock

What is it about chicken stock? A bowl of it with a couple of twists of a pepper mill, and you've got homemade medicine. Once you make chicken stock, you will never go back to canned. Don't salt and pepper the stock until the next day. After you have removed the fat, heat the stock, add a little salt and pepper and proceed with any recipe.

3 pounds chicken bones (raw)

3 stalks celery cut in large pieces

2 carrots cut in large pieces

1 onion cut in large pieces

1 bay leaf

8 whole black pepper corns

Cover all ingredients with cold water and bring to a boil in a large stockpot. Skim foam as it forms on top. Simmer for 2 hours. Strain stock and chill before use. All of the fat will solidify on top after stock is cold. Simply pull off fat and use for sauté.

Brown Beef Stock

Ask any friendly butcher for some beef bones to make stock. The cost will be nominal. To make a super concentrated stock, a kind of demi-glace, after straining reduce stock simmering several hours until the stock is dark, somewhat thickened and shinny. Freeze in ice cube trays and pop out to use for a quick sauce.

1 pounds beef bones

1 small can tomato paste

3 stalks celery cut in large pieces

2 carrots cut in large pieces

1 onion cut in large pieces

3 cups red wine

1 bay leaf

10 whole black peppercorns

1 bunch of fresh herbs (tied together)

To make a great brown stock you must have a large roasting pan and a heavy bottomed stockpot. Place the bones, celery, carrot, and onion in the roasting pan. Spread the tomato paste over the bones and the stock vegetables. Place in a 400° oven for 45 minutes to 1 hour. Place pan on top of the stove and with tongs place the bones and the stock vegetables in the stockpot. Cover with water. Turn heat on high under roasting pan. Add wine and cook, scraping all the particles (the goodie) off the pan. Add to stockpot. Add bay leaf, peppercorns and herbs. Bring to a boil. Skim off foam as it forms. Turn down to a simmer for 5-8 hours. Strain and cool in refrigerator overnight. After stock is cold, remove fat from stock by lifting it off the top. Use fat for roasting new potatoes with fresh rosemary, salt and pepper.

Gravy

The official sauce of the Deep-South. The southern sauce for sopping. You can make this milk gravy by, replacing the stock with milk, use pan drippings for the butter. After the milk gravy is thickened add crumbled, cooked sausage. If the gravy is too thick, thin with milk or stock.

2 Tablespoons butter

½ small onion (diced small)

4 Tablespoons flour

1 teaspoon poultry rub

4 cups chicken stock

salt and pepper

Sauté onion in butter until soft. Add flour and cook 2-3 minutes. Add poultry rub. Add stock and bring to a boil. Reduce heat and simmer 5-10 minutes. Salt and pepper to taste. If you want to make a beef gravy use beef rub and beef stock in place of poultry rub and chicken stock.

Poultry Rub

I developed this recipe for turkeys and chickens. Rub bird inside and out and rest over night in refrigerator. Another trick is the night before, soak the bird in a pot of water with 1 cup of kosher salt. Place pot in refrigerator. The next day drain salt water and rinse chicken in cold water. Pat dry and rub with poultry rub. Continue any recipe.

3 Tablespoons dried sage

1 Tablespoon sugar

1 Tablespoon Kosher salt

1 Tablespoon paprika

1 Tablespoon black pepper

1 Tablespoon dried lemon zest (optional)

Blend and keep in air-tight container.

Beef Rub

A dry rub sounds strange at first but I know you will be surprised at the results. Use latex exam gloves to rub the dry mixture into the meat, like you were giving a Shiatsu massage to a loved one.

3 Tablespoons coriander

1 Tablespoon Kosher salt

1 Tablespoon black pepper

1 Tablespoon sugar

1 teaspoon oregano

1 teaspoon thyme

1 teaspoon cayenne pepper

1 teaspoon rosemary

Blend together and store in air-tight container.

Beef Marinade

This is a simple marinade, best used for smoking meats.

2 quarts soy sauce

2 onions sliced thin

1 head of garlic crushed with a mallet

½ cup fresh oregano chopped with stems

2 sprigs fresh rosemary chopped

Combine all ingredients and pour over beef. Marinate for 12 hours. Whole prime ribs will take 24 hours. If you are marinating steaks, do so for only 1 hour. If you are marinating whole tenderloins, cut soy in half and add same amount of water. Discard marinade after use.

Red Eye Gravy

This one gets its name from its invention. Someone that just woke up and had red eyes for one reason or another, cooked some ham or sausage and deglaze the pan with coffee. That is basically it. During the Depression they would use shredded lettuce to give the gravy some body. This is a simple and authentic recipe.

2 center cut slices of smoked ham

1 cup of coffee

1 tablespoon flour

pepper and a little salt

Brown the ham slices on both sides. Remove from pan. Sprinkle the flour in the pan and scrape pan. Add the hot coffee and stir. Allow to cook for 2-3 minutes. Pour over ham.

Homemade Catchup

If you are going to use catchup, make your own. Tomato catchup is a condiment developed from the original, mushroom catchup. A type of spiced mushroom sauce. This tomato catchup lasts for 2 weeks in an air tight container in the refrigerator.

3 to 6 pounds tomatoes

4 to 5 onions (peeled and sliced)

5 cloves garlic

2 jalapeno peppers (whole)

2 bay leaves

1 Tablespoon Kosher salt

1 Tablespoon allspice

1 Tablespoon celery seed

1 Tablespoon caraway seeds

1 Tablespoon coriander seeds

1 teaspoon cayenne pepper

2 sticks cinnamon

¾ cup sugar

2 cups red wine vinegar

Sir Robert "Chef Bob" Vaningan O.S.C.

Bring first 6 ingredients to a boil for 10-15 minutes, and strain through a sieve. Add spices and sugar and cook, stirring occasionally until thickened. Add the vinegar and cook an additional 10-15 minutes. Strain through a sieve, store in glass or plastic containers. Preserve by canning according to manufacturer's directions.

Cocktail Sauce

A condiment for boiled shrimp or fried fish.

1 cup Tomato catchup

1 Tablespoon fresh lemon juice

1 teaspoon lime juice

1 Tablespoon horseradish

6 drops hot sauce

salt and pepper

Combine ingredients and store in plastic or glass, refrigerated.

Sir Robert "Chef Bob" Vaningan O.S.C.

Poppy Seed Dip

Make a batch of this dip and store in refrigerator for up to 2 weeks. I use this recipe with fruit, as a dip or a fruit dressing.

1 cup sour cream

1 cup plain yogurt

1 cup sugar

2 Tablespoons grenadine syrup

1 Tablespoon poppy seeds

Mix all ingredients. Rest in refrigerator for 1 hour. Mix again and serve.

Pork Marinade

Do not marinate pork too long or it will pickle and be tough.

1 cup cider vinegar

1 cup brown sugar

¾ cup soy sauce

2 teaspoons crushed red pepper flakes

5 cloves garlic chopped

1 Tablespoon chopped ginger

Mix all ingredients. Marinate pork loins or pork butts. Marinate overnight.

Cranberry Sauce

There should be no reason to buy canned cranberry sauce except out of convenience. Once you have made this recipe you will not look at canned the same again. Cranberries have a lot of natural pectin and jells almost immediately.

1 package fresh cranberries

1 cup sugar

2 cups cranberry juice

Pick through cranberries, discarding the bad ones. Place them into a heavy bottomed saucepan. Add sugar and juice. Bring to a boil. Skim foam that develops and cook until berries pop and thicken. Preserve by home canning method described by manufacture's instructions. Make a double or triple batch and you will have enough for gifts, holidays, and the occasional midnight turkey sandwich.

BBQ Sauce

Everyone you know has the best BBQ sauce recipe in the world, so they tell you. Surprise the host of a back yard BBQ with this sauce as a gift and they will say that <u>you</u> have the best BBQ sauce recipe (in the world). This sauce is perfect for first time home canning enthusiast.

2 cups red chili sauce

3 cups ketchup

1 cup Worcestershire sauce

1 cup red wine vinegar

1 pound dark brown sugar

2 Tablespoons BBQ spice

1 Tablespoon oregano leaves

1 ½ teaspoons crushed red pepper flakes

Bring all ingredients to a boil in a heavy bottomed pot, simmer for 1 hour stirring occasionally. Store in glass or plastic container.

Sir Robert "Chef Bob" Vaningan O.S.C.

Chocolate Sauce

If you can't get enough chocolate, make this sauce and pour it over whatever.

½ cup of chopped chocolate (bitter-sweet)

½ cup hot coffee (strong coffee preferred)

Chop chocolate and place in a medium size mixing bowl. Boil coffee and whisk into the chocolate. Serve warm.

Ganache

French filling that can be used for a lot of recipes. Icing, truffles, cake and cookie filling, the list is endless.

24 ounces semi-sweet chocolate

2 cups of heavy cream

Place chopped chocolate in a medium mixing bowl. Bring the heavy cream to a boil, pour over chocolate. Shake bowl so that the hot cream seeps down into the chocolate. Rest for 5 minutes. Stir with a whisk until mixture is smooth.

Southern Sweet and Sour Sauce

A perfect balance of hot, sweet and sour. Store this sauce in glass or plastic.

1-8 ounce jar apple jelly

1-8 ounce jar pineapple preserves

½ cup spicy brown mustard

1-8 ounce jar horseradish

1 cup apple juice

2 jalapenos chopped (seeds removed)

Heat all ingredients to a boil in a non stick pan. This is one of the best sauces for pork.

Roasted Garlic Mayonnaise

Making your own mayonnaise is simple and very delicious. The addition of roasted garlic brings a depth of flavor unmatched by anything else you could add.

5 heads garlic

2 cups salad oil

2 teaspoons salt

1 Tablespoon Dijon mustard

1/8 teaspoon cayenne pepper

2 egg yolks

¼ cup apple cider vinegar

Place whole garlic and oil in a heat proof bowl, cover with foil and bake for 45 minutes to 1 hour at 350°. Allow to cool to room temperature. Remove garlic from oil, cut off root end and squeeze garlic into a mixing bowl or a blender. Combine mustard, salt, pepper, and egg yolks with the roasted garlic. Begin whisking quickly, adding a few drops of vinegar at a time. Begin adding garlic infused oil a few drops at a time. If you are using a blender, keep machine running while adding vinegar and oil. Alternate vinegar and oil in this fashion until you have a beautiful, roasted garlic mayonnaise.

Tartar Sauce

Once you have mastered the art of mayonnaise making, you can make a variety of mayonnaise based sauces. This is my version of the most famous.

1 cup roasted garlic mayonnaise

2 Tablespoons fine diced onion

1 Tablespoon capers

1 Tablespoon diced pickles

1 Tablespoon fresh lemon juice

salt and pepper

Combine all ingredients and refrigerate. Use with **fried catfish** and **hushpuppies (see index).**

Blue Cheese Dressing

I love blue cheese. I have eaten some of the best in the world, with walnuts, grapes, and a glass of Sambucco with a hot coffee bean floating in the snifter. I think you will enjoy using this recipe as a dressing or as a dip.

2 cups roasted garlic mayonnaise

½ small purple onion (minced)

½ cup or more crumbled (good blue cheese)

2 lemons juiced

2 cloves garlic chopped

½ teaspoon salt

½ teaspoon pepper

2 Tablespoons basil chopped (or 2 teaspoons dried)

½ to 1 cup of milk

Mix all in order. Store in glass or plastic in the refrigerator, lasts 2 weeks if you don't eat it all before then.

Cheese Sauce

This sauce can be used for 100 ideas. You decide what to use it with. In this book I have used this sauce with **Oysters Florentine** and **Macaroni and Cheese (see index)**.

5 cups milk

½ cup blonde roux

salt and pepper

1 cup shredded cheese

¼ cup parmesan (grated)

1/8 teaspoon paprika

Bring milk to a boil, lower heat to simmer. Whisk in roux and bring back to a boil over high heat. Be careful not to let the pot boil over. Whisk so as not to burn sauce. After sauce has thickened, 3-5 minutes, take off heat and whisk in cheeses. Add salt and pepper. I like to add a pinch of cayenne and a pinch of paprika. Do not bring back to a boil.

Pecan Sauce

This sauce is great for ice cream. Store in air-tight container in refrigerator.

3 cups heavy cream

2 cups brown sugar

1 stick butter

¾ cup corn syrup

2 cups pecan pieces

In a pot, reduce cream by half. In another pot mix remaining ingredients and bring to a boil. Add reduced cream and keep warm.

Chapter 5
Soups and Stews

Sir Robert "Chef Bob" Vaningan O.S.C.

<u>Chapter 5</u>

Soups and Stews

In a world of hospitality like the Deep-South, soups and stews are a staple that is frequently made and some always given away to a friend or neighbor. The recipes I have developed for you in this chapter will give your family and friends years of great comfort food. Freezing soups and stews will make quick dinners easier. One-pot meals have been around since fire and pots, but the basic idea is to build flavors by starting with cooking the onions, garlic, celery and carrots, if any. Then adding other ingredients a little at a time and season with whatever herb, salt and pepper. Taste often. You can always add salt and pepper but it is very difficult to take away. Try to use homemade stocks when ever possible and remember to taste often. Invest in a good heavy bottomed pot for soup making. 15 to 20 quart should be perfect.

Chicken Soup

Chicken Soup

I love soup for dinner. I seem to sleep better after a humble bowl. Nothing is as noble and at the same time as common as chicken soup. We take it to the sick and they recover. It's homemade medicine in a pot. This is yet another recipe that is a perfect freezer friendly food, and you will be so happy to know that you have some wonderful soup in the freezer readily available in minutes.

1- 2 to 3 pound chicken (well salted and peppered)

Stock vegetables *

1 onion (diced)

2 stalks of celery (strung and diced)

1 carrot (peeled and diced)

¼ cup canola oil

¼ cup flour

2 teaspoons fresh thyme leaves

salt and pepper

1 lemon

2-3 quarts water or stock

In a medium size pot, place the salted and peppered chicken (whole or cut up). Add the stock vegetables,* cover with water. Bring to a boil, turn the heat to a simmer. Skim the foamy surface and allow to cook for 45 minutes to one hour. After 30 minutes of simmering the chicken, sauté onion, celery, and carrot in the canola oil, using a separate, large, heavy bottomed pot. After vegetables are somewhat soft, add the flour and stir with a whisk until well blended. Cook only 2 to 3 minutes. Do not brown. Remove chicken from stock and allow to drain on a sheet pan. Strain stock into sautéed vegetables and flour mixture. Add the thyme. Stir with a whisk and bring to a boil. Add the juice and rind of the lemon, into the soup. Pull the chicken meat off the bone and cut into smaller pieces, then add to the soup. Bring to a boil again. Taste for seasoning and if you are suffering from a cold, add 2-3 twists of a peppermill to your bowl. The extra pepper will help open your sinuses.

Stock vegetables* = 1 small onion, 2 small carrot, 3 stalks celery (rough cut)

Georgian Peanut and Chicken Soup

Who discovered the peanut? There are debates about it, but we do know that George Washington Carver made the peanut famous. Remember that peanuts are legumes, not really nuts. You will love this soup. Serve with **banana bread (see index)** toast.

2 stalks celery (strung and chopped)

1 onion (chopped)

1 carrot (peeled and chopped)

4 Tablespoons peanut oil

3 Tablespoons flour

5 cups chicken stock

1 ¼ cups peanut butter

1 cup heavy cream

1 pound cooked chicken

½ cup chopped peanuts

Sauté onions, carrot, and celery in the peanut oil. When vegetables are soft add flour and stir with a whisk. Add chicken stock and bring to a boil. Add peanut butter and cream. Bring to a boil stirring. Add cooked chicken and bring back to a boil. Stir one more time. If this soup is too thick just thin with milk, cream, or stock.

Chicken and Dumplings

One of the Deep South's gifts to the world; Chicken and Dumplings. Fundamentally it is a chicken soup with big, fat noodles. Imagine it's freezing outside and you are hungry. That's all the motivation it will take for you to make this recipe. This is one of my recipes that you should make ahead and freeze in 2 to 4 portions so that you can put together a fast and satisfying, great meal.

1 large chicken cut up in pieces (skin removed)

*Stock vegetables

1 onion cut in large dice

1 stalk celery, cut in large dice

1 carrot peeled and cut in large dice

8-10 cups chicken stock (more may be required)

Bring to a boil and simmer for 1 hour the stock, chicken, and stock vegetables. Make sure chicken is cooked thoroughly. Remove chicken and allow to cool on a cookie sheet. Strain out the stock vegetables. Clean pot and begin sautéing the onion celery and carrot in oil until slightly softened. Try not to brown. Add strained stock into sautéed vegetables.

*Stock Vegetables = 1 onion, 1 carrot, 1 stalk of celery, rough cut.

Dumplings

2 cups plain flour

½ cup shortening

salt and pepper

1 cup chicken stock (more or less)

Sift flour in a medium bowl. Cut in shortening as for biscuits. Add salt, pepper and chicken stock. Mix dough with a wooden spoon or heavy metal spoon. Do not work dough too much. Roll out on a floured surface about 1/4 inch thick. Cut in strips about 3 inches wide and 4-5 inches long. Place on a cookie sheet and place in the freezer for at least 1 hour. Remove chicken from the bones and set aside. Taste stock and see if you need more salt and pepper. Bring stock to a boil and add dumplings, two or three at a time until all the dumplings are used. Cook for 7 minutes. Keep stock simmering. Add chicken. For a thicker recipe add 5-6 Tablespoons of roux to the boiling stock.

* For fluffy dumplings add 2 teaspoons baking powder and 1 egg to dumpling recipe and scoop with a spoon into stock.

Cream of Tomato Soup

4 ripe tomatoes

1 small onion (diced)

3 cloves garlic (chopped)

1 red bell pepper (chopped)

3 Tablespoons olive oil

1 sprig fresh thyme

1 sprig fresh rosemary

1 quart chicken stock or vegetable stock

1 cup heavy cream

5 drops of hot sauce

Sauté onion, pepper and garlic in olive oil until soft. Cut tomatoes in half and remove vine end and as many seeds as you can. Cut tomatoes in 3 or 4 pieces and add to pot. Cook tomatoes for 2-3 minutes stirring occasionally. Add thyme and chicken or vegetable stock. Cook simmering for 10-15 minutes. Puree soup and adjust seasoning with salt, pepper and hot sauce. Add cream and heat soup to serve, or serve cold by omitting the cream and using tomato juice.

Corn and Crab Chowder

When I was 15 I had a life moment experience of catching crabs in the back-water bay of south Alabama. We were cooking and picking crabs that we had caught that day, when a guy called us and was screaming on the phone, "JUBILEE! JUBILEE!" My cousin told me to "grab a net and a cooler!" I did as I was commanded and ran as fast as I could behind him in the dark toward the bay. We arrived in a matter of minutes, to my disbelief, hundreds of south Alabamians were all doing the same thing, jumping into the black water that looked as if it was boiling. Then I saw the miracle, people scooping the water with their nets and filling ice chests with very alive crabs. "What's happening?" I asked. And the reply was, "don't just stand there, jump in, jubilee only lasts a few minutes." I jumped in, tennis shoes still on and ice chest in tow. I had to go as deep as my underarms, where the action was taking place. I was almost in shock. I could feel the crabs tickling my sides, like a swarm of giant, aquatic spiders. The crabs were dancing on top of the water in the moonlight as far as I could see, and hundreds of people with lanterns and nets were wading into the bay. It looked like a scene from the movie **Titanic**, over a hundred heads of people bobbing in the water, yelling out to each other in the dark. I was scared and excited at the same time. I did what everybody else was doing, filling my ice chest. In about 10 minutes the spectacle was over and I had an ice chest full of excited, bay blue crabs. Later I learned this was a not frequent occurrence, and could only be explained as a gift from GOD. I think of that night every time I eat crab.

Enjoy this chowder, hot or cold.

1 small onion diced

2 stalks celery

1 stick butter

¼ cup flour

5 ears of corn (kernels removed)

3 potatoes (diced skin on)

6 cups chicken stock or (crab stock)

1 Tablespoon old bay seasoning

salt and pepper

1 cup heavy cream

1 pound jumbo lump crab meat

Sauté onion and celery in butter. Add flour and cook 3-4 minutes. Add potatoes and stock. Cook until potatoes are tender. Add corn and cook for 10 minutes. Add all other ingredients and adjust seasoning with salt and pepper. This is very hearty and so good in the winter months.

Alabama Gumbo

Louisiana is not the only place in the world to find gumbo. Gumbo is an African word (Kumba) from either Swahili or Bantu meaning okra. The okra gives this soup body. In the Deep South we like to use ground sassafras leaves in our gumbo, also adding thickness and flavor. The first thing you need to do is make a brown roux. (see below).

1 chicken (cooked and pulled off bone)

2 cups smoked sausage (diced)

1 pound shrimp (peeled)

1 pound crab meat (jumbo lump)

1 onion diced

10 cloves garlic chopped

1 bell pepper diced

2 stalks celery diced

1 carrot (peeled and diced)

1 stick butter

8 cups chicken stock

½ to ¾ cup brown roux

1 ½ cups sliced okra

Sir Robert "Chef Bob" Vaningan O.S.C.

1 teaspoon dry mustard

1 bay leaf

1 teaspoon file' (ground sassafras)

salt and pepper

Make a brown roux first (see below). In a large heavy bottomed pot, sauté vegetables in butter for 2-3 minutes. Add chicken stock and bring to a boil. Add roux and whisk until stock comes back to a boil. It must come to a boil and then simmer for at least 20 minutes. Begin adding all of the remaining ingredients except crabmeat. The crab is so delicate it must be the last thing you add to the gumbo. Now it's time to taste the gumbo and adjust seasoning. Serve with rice.

Brown Roux

To make a brown roux, start with the **roux** recipe.

2 sticks butter

1 cup flour

Continue cooking the roux until it begins to turn brown. You must stir continuously. To keep from burning roux remove from heat often as you continue to stir. Place back on the heat source and continue to stir until desired brown color is achieved. The more brown the roux, the better the flavor, but the less thickening power it has. Another trick is to brown the flour on a sheet pan, mix with melted butter or oil. Feel free to add or subtract any of the meats in this recipe. You can then rename the recipe California gumbo, or Maine gumbo, or Iowa gumbo, you get the idea.

Clam Chowder

Ok, clam chowder isn't really Deep South cuisine, but we do have some clams that come out of the Gulf of Mexico. And I did train under a chef from Boston, so I think you will love this recipe.

1 small onion (diced)

4 cloves garlic

3 stalks celery (diced)

1 stick butter

3 ounces salt pork (diced)

¼ cup flour

3 potatoes (diced skin on)

2-12 ounce cans of chopped clams

1 cup milk

Salt and pepper

Sauté onion, celery and garlic in butter and diced salt pork. After vegetables are soft stir in flour and cook 2-3 minutes. Add potatoes and milk. Bring to a boil and then simmer for 15 minutes. Add clams and clam juice. Adjust seasoning with salt and pepper.

Oyster Stew

Apalachicola, Alabama, <u>the</u> place for oysters in the Deep South. There are probably 10 or 20 recipes I could write for you using oysters. This stew has been around me for 40 years, I hope you enjoy it.

3 to 4 green onions (chopped)

1 small stalk celery (diced small)

4 cloves garlic (chopped)

1 stick butter

3 Tablespoons flour

3 cups milk

2 cups half and half

1 pint oysters in their liquor

salt and pepper

1 to 6 drops hot sauce

Saltine crackers or hard crusted French bread

(one must)

Sauté onions, celery, and garlic in butter until soft but not brown. Add flour and cook 2 to 3 minutes. Add milk and half and half. Stir and cook until stew comes to a boil, then turn down to a simmer. In a large nonstick pan heat oysters in their own liquor until the edges of oysters begin to curl. Add oysters and liquor to stew. Turn off stew, you do not want it to boil again. Serve immediately.

Real Chili

What is real chili? You will probably have to go to Texas to find that out. Cowboys are the forefathers of chili. Early Southwestern cowboys, with spices from Mexico, created a stew to preserve cubes of beef on the trail. The use of hot peppers (chilies) and spices, cumin, cilantro, salt and pepper were used in large quantities to hide the taste of older meat. The addition of black beans and sometimes potatoes were added to make it a meal. Everyone has their own version of chili. This is the one I like to use.

1 large onion (chopped)

10 cloves garlic (chopped)

1 small carrot (peeled and chopped)

6 green onions (chopped)

4 fresh jalapenos (diced)

2 tomatoes (diced)

6 strips smoked bacon (cubed)

3 Tablespoons vegetable oil

3 pounds beef tips (tenderloin trimmings preferred)

1 quart water or beef stock

1 pound dried black beans

1 bunch fresh cilantro (chopped)

1 Tablespoon cumin

3 Tablespoons chili powder

2 teaspoons black pepper

2 teaspoons cayenne pepper

2 teaspoons salt

additional salt and pepper to adjust seasoning

In a large heavy bottomed pot cook the bacon in the 3 Tablespoons of oil until the bacon is cooked and rendered of most of its fat. Cook the first six ingredients in this oil and fat combination until softened. Brown the beef tips in the pot with the vegetables. Add the water or stock and the dried beans. Make sure the beans are covered with enough liquid to cook them properly. Bring to a boil and simmer for 1 hour, adding more water or stock if needed. Add remaining ingredients after the first 30 minutes of cooking. Continue cooking until the black beans are tender. You may want to soak the black beans for 2 to 3 hours before you begin the recipe. This will make cooking time shorter. Taste your chili and adjust seasoning to your liking. Omit the jalapenos and cayenne pepper for a mild chili.

Poppy Gosh

My cousins, siblings, and I grew up eating this type of quick stew, although no one in our family knows where it came from or who started it, I found out through research that it dates back to early Cuba. I just know it's quick and easy and tastes very good.

1 onion (chopped)

3 cloves garlic

3 Tablespoons olive oil

1 cup red wine

2 tomatoes (diced or canned diced)

1 jalapeno pepper (chopped)

4 potatoes (cubed, skin on)

2 pounds chopped sirloin or (or ground chuck))

2 lemons (fresh and cut in half)

2 sprigs fresh thyme or (1 teaspoon dried thyme)

salt & pepper

water or stock to cover ingredients in pot

Sauté onions and garlic in oil until soft, add the chopped sirloin and brown. Drain excess grease, add 1 cup red wine, and all other ingredients. Be sure to squeeze as much juice from the lemons as possible into the pot, straining out the seeds. Drop in the lemons, yes, peel and all. After covering ingredients with water or stock bring to a boil, simmer until potatoes are done, about 30 minutes. Adjust seasoning with salt and pepper. Serve with rice if desired.

Venison Stew

During hunting season, some of my customers bring portions of their venison to me. This is the stew I like to make with leg or shoulder meat.

1/2 cup oil

1/2 cup flour

salt and pepper to season flour

3 pounds venison (cut in cubes, then pounded with a meat mallet)

Pound venison between two pieces of plastic wrap. Pound enough to break down the tissue. Do not pound into hamburger. Dredge pounded venison in seasoned flour and brown in oil. Remove browned venison to a plate.

4 Tablespoons oil (if needed)

1 large onion (diced)

2 carrots (peeled and diced)

2 celery stalks (diced)

5 cloves garlic (minced)

4 Tablespoons flour

1 cup wild mushrooms (chopped)

1 cup red wine

1 sprig rosemary

4 juniper berries (crushed)

1 teaspoon crushed red pepper

2 bay leaves

1 quart venison stock or water

salt and pepper

1 cup red wine (for chef to drink while stew is simmering)

Sauté onions, carrots, celery and garlic in remaining browning oil. You may need to add the 4 tablespoons of oil. Add the mushrooms and cook 2-3 minutes. Add the flour. Cook and stir 2-3 minutes. Add the red wine and deglaze the pot by scraping all the goodie (browned particles from the bottom of the pot.) Add remaining ingredients. Add venison. Bring to a boil. Add more liquid if necessary. Turn down to a simmer, cover with foil and place in oven at 375° for 2 to 3 hours. If your pot will not fit, simmer on top of the stove for 1 to 2 hours until meat is tender. If all liquid seems to be absorbing add a little more stock or water. Stir occasionally. Taste often between sips of red wine.

Rabbit Stew

I remember when I was twelve, an old Norwegian man named Clarence, taught me how to run a trap line. My favorite book to read was **Trap Lines North** by Stephen W. Meader. I was in a world of my own. I loved setting the traps and in a day or two walking the 2 hour hike and seeing if the trap doors were shut. What a heart pounding experience to walk up to a homemade box trap and peek inside, not knowing what you will find. Sometimes it would be an owl or a blue jay or a raccoon. I have to admit it took me a while to get the hang of grabbing a wild rabbit and actually killing and butchering it. This is the first time I have told anyone but, I let at least 20 to 30 rabbits go in the beginning of my trapping career. Hey! I was twelve. I told my parents there just weren't any rabbits those days, or they escaped. Soon I got the hang of it and I was bringing home 4 or 5 rabbits almost every day. I think my mom made every kind of rabbit dish that year. What a wonderful bounty God has provided us in nature. I would strongly suggest raising your own or buying farm raised FDA approved rabbits. Most grocery stores now carry frozen rabbits. Allow rabbit to thaw in refrigerator, then proceeded with recipe.

2 rabbits cleaned and cut in pieces

2 cups flour

2 teaspoons salt

1 teaspoon black pepper

¼ cup canola oil

1 stick butter

1 onion (diced)

2 stalks celery (diced)

2 carrots (peeled and diced)

1 bell pepper (diced)

2 cups wild mushrooms (or domestic)

1 cup chopped tomato (deseeded)

2 cups red wine

1 sprig fresh rosemary

2 sprigs fresh sage chopped (2 teaspoons rubbed sage)

2 bay leaves

8 cups stock or water

salt and pepper to taste

Heat oil and butter in a heavy bottomed pot. Mix salt and pepper with flour. Season rabbit pieces with salt and pepper, dredge in flour and brown in oil, butter mixture. Remove rabbit to a holding platter and cook onions, celery, carrots, and bell pepper until softened. Add mushrooms and tomato, cook until some of the mushroom liquid is released. Add red wine and scrape the goodie (browned particles stuck to the bottom of the pot.). Add herbs and stock or water, bring to a boil and taste. Add just a small amount of salt and pepper. Add rabbit pieces and simmer for 1 to 2 hours or until rabbit is tender. Add more stock or water if needed. Taste and adjust with salt and pepper.

Chef Bob & Papa Marc

Chapter 6
Chow-Chows, Pickles, and Relishes

Morgan & Summer Water Melon

Chapter 6

<u>Chow-Chows, Pickles, and Relishes</u>

This is a fun and simple chapter. The recipes in this chapter are designed for preserving, and are great accompaniments to many foods. Relishes and pickles add to any meal with color, texture and pungent tastes. Chow-Chow is kind of like a pickled relish. Why is it called Chow-Chow? My professional opinion is it came from Chinese immigrants. Chow mein means ends and pieces. I can only imagine that chopped ends and pieces of cabbage, peppers, and onions were pickled and preserved. Invest in some home canning equipment and follow instructions provided by the manufacturer. Use non reactive pots (stainless steel). Do not use aluminum. Use your imagination, pickle whatever you like.

Chef Bob's Chow-Chow

This is a recipe I developed from a mustard slaw recipe. This is a must for BBQ. Stir with a long handled spoon quite often to prevent burning. Keep refrigerated and this chow-chow will keep for weeks.

1 large cabbage (chopped)

1 bell pepper (chopped)

1 large onion (chopped)

2 carrots (chopped)

1 can corn (drained)

2 cups plain mustard

1 ½ cups ketchup

1 cup vinegar

2 cups sugar

1 Tablespoon salt

2 teaspoons black pepper

½ teaspoon cayenne pepper

Place all ingredients, except cabbage, in a heavy bottomed, large pot. Bring to a boil. Add cabbage and bring back to a boil, then simmer for 5-10 minutes. Store in glass or plastic. This relish will keep a long time if air tight and refrigerated. This recipe is great for home canning.

Old Fashioned Chow-Chow

Chow chow? What does it mean? The Chinese chow mein means ends and pieces. I'm going to guess that's how this famous relish got its' name.

2 heads green cabbage (chopped)

6 hard green tomatoes (chopped)

3 green bell peppers (chopped)

3 red bell peppers (chopped)

2 large jalapeno peppers (chopped)

10 onions (chopped)

5 Stalks celery (chopped)

1 cup kosher salt

2 quarts vinegar

3 cups sugar

6 Tablespoons dry mustard

3 Tablespoons mustard seeds

1 Tablespoon crushed red pepper

1 Tablespoon celery seed

1 bay leaf

Mix vegetables and layer with kosher salt, using a large plastic pail or stainless steel bowl. Let stand over night at room temperature. Drain well in a plastic or stainless colander. Bring vinegar to a boil with sugar, dry mustard, red pepper, mustard seeds, celery seed, and bay leaf. Add all ingredients and cook for 20-30 minutes. Great for home canning.

Apple Relish

This recipe will give you years of great gift giving and something different to go with pork or poultry. Don't over cook the apples or you will have, apple relish butter. Always pick hard, unblemished green apples. If you can get organic, non-waxed green apples you can leave the peel on.

14 green apples (peeled and diced)

4 jalapeno peppers (diced)

3 purple onions (diced)

3 cups apple cider vinegar

1 cup sugar

3 cinnamon sticks (broken)

Cook in a heavy bottomed pot over high heat for 8-10 minutes. Fill glass jars and process according to canning instructions.

Apple Butter

In hard Deep-South times any real butter that was made was more valuable to sell or trade rather than eat. So, this apple spread was used instead of butter, (apple butter).

12 peeled and chopped apples (red baking apples)

5 ½ cups sugar

½ cup apple cider vinegar

½ cup apple cider

1 teaspoon salt

½ teaspoon cayenne pepper

1 teaspoon cinnamon

Mix all ingredients in a heavy bottomed pot. Bring to a boil and simmer for 2-3 hours. Make sure you stir often to prevent burning. For a more smooth apple butter allow to cool and then pass through a food mill.

Pickled Pumpkin

You will love this recipe. October and November produces tons of pumpkins. Besides the great roasted pumpkin and the famed pumpkin pie, this is the best use of the beautiful orange squash.

4 ½ pounds pumpkin (peeled and cut into 1 inch cubes)

1 stick of cinnamon (broken)

1 teaspoon whole cloves

1 teaspoon crushed red pepper

1 teaspoon Kosher salt

4 cups vinegar

3 ½ pounds sugar

Add vinegar and sugar to a heavy bottomed pot. Add spices and cook for 5-8 minutes. Add pumpkin and cook until pumpkin is tender. Place in sterile jars and cover pumpkin with any leftover syrup. Seal jars according to manufactures instructions.

Squash Pickles

8 cups squash (sliced ½ inch)

2 cups onions (sliced thin)

2 jalapenos (whole)

2 Tablespoons kosher salt

2 cups cider vinegar

3 ½ cups sugar

1 Tablespoon mustard seed

2 bay leaves

1 Tablespoon black peppercorns

1 sprig fresh rosemary

Combine all ingredients and bring to a boil. Store in glass or plastic container. Preserve in canning jars according to manufactures direction.

Brandied Peaches

Brandied peaches are one of my favorite cohorts for baked ham and sweet potato casserole. Use large, firm, clingstone peaches.

3 pounds peaches (peeled)

6 cups sugar

1 teaspoon whole cloves

3 cinnamon sticks

4 cups water

6 cups brandy (good quality)

Tie cloves and cinnamon in a piece of cheesecloth. Bring the sugar, water and spices to a boil for 5 minutes. Drop whole, peeled, peaches into syrup a few at a time and cook till tender but not too soft. Repeat until all peaches are finished. Drain peaches on a plate or cookie sheet. Place whole, drained peaches in sterile jars. Pour syrup from drained peaches back into syrup pot. Cook syrup until reduced and thickened. Allow syrup to cool completely, then mix in brandy and cover peaches. Seal jars according to manufactures directions. Try not to drink too much of the peach brandy, if you can.

Watermelon Rind Pickles

Watermelon is another one of Africa's gorgeous contributions to the Deep-South. We eat watermelon like, well, like water. Imagine a 30-pound watermelon that has been iced down in an ice chest for 2 days, the thermometer on the pecan tree reads 102°. All of your friends and relatives are having fun out in the hot Alabama sun and everyone has finished eating fried chicken, catfish, hushpuppies, grilled ribs and God knows what else. The ice cream is churning and now it's time to cut the watermelon. Usually an older member of the family takes the honored position, because no one else knows how to cut a watermelon. (You have to be at least 45 to be able to master the fine art of cutting such a prize.) The melon is lifted on the wooden picnic table, resting on old newspapers, and the honored melon cutting master looks at everyone with a reverenced nod and pushes the knife into the shinny, dark green skin. The crowd is silenced for a second or two as a loud splitting sound separates the perfect melon into 2 halves. The red flesh is dotted with black seeds and as each person is handed a perfect specimen. The knowledgeable watermelon eater will take the familiar watermelon stance, legs apart, bent over, elbows out, mouth agape, salt shaker in hand, and only then can you bite into the ice cold sweet melon. Don't worry about the seeds. Leave them in your mouth so you can line up for the seed-spiting contest. Gather up all the rinds and wash them well. Peel the dark green skin and any red melon flesh. You are now ready to make watermelon rind pickles.

9 cups watermelon rind cubes (dark green peel removed)

3 Tablespoons fresh lime juice

1 cup cider vinegar

3 cups sugar

2 teaspoons kosher salt

3 cinnamon sticks

1 teaspoon crushed red pepper

1 quart cider vinegar

Add watermelon rind cubes, lime juice, salt, and enough water to cover cubes into a plastic container. Let stand overnight at room temperature. The next day, drain and rinse rinds. Place rinds in a heavy bottomed pot and cover cubes with water. Break cinnamon sticks into pot and cook for 40-50 minutes. Add sugar and vinegar to water melon cubes in the heavy bottomed pot. Cook until a thick syrup develops. Let stand again over night in a glass or stainless bowl. Divide into glass jars and fill to the top. Bring 1 quart of cider vinegar to a boil and add a little to each jar. Process as instructed by home canning method, provided by manufacturer.

Nathan & Morgan

Chapter 7
Perfect Meats

Prime Rib

Chapter 7

Perfect Meats

I took my time writing this chapter for you to insure ease and simplicity. I want you to be comfortable trying all of my recipes. Please don't skip a recipe because it sounds difficult.

"If you can read, you can cook." A quote from a good friend David Tanner.

Perfect Meats

Mattie and her Fish

Roast Beef

A simple understated centerpiece for the dinner table. Buy a choice or prime rib, still on the bone (Black Angus preferred). Plan your dinner to be served 1 hour after roast is finished cooking, to allow a rest before carving. This is very important so the roast can relax and hold all of its' wonderful juices.

1 10-12 pound prime rib (on the bone preferred)

6 whole heads of garlic

4 large onions

2 carrots

3 stalks of celery

1 cup Kosher salt (yes, 1 cup)

6 Tablespoons crushed black peppercorns

1 ½ bottles of red wine or water or stock

Cut onions in half and place cut side down in a roasting pan. Add the whole garlic heads, then rough cut carrots and celery and place in bottom of pan. This will be the vegetable raft the roast will rest on while cooking. Place roast on top of vegetable raft, bone side down. Make crosscut slits in the beef fat and pour bottle of red wine over roast. Cover with salt and pepper. Roast in slow oven 300° for 35 minutes per pound. Allow to rest 1 hour on a platter after roasting time is over. Take roast from oven and remove to a resting platter. Don't forget to allow roast to rest 45 minutes to 1 hour. Place roasting pan on top of stove on high heat and add 1/2 bottle of red wine to pan, scraping the goodie (browned partials of caramelized vegetables, from the bottom.) After scraping is finished, strain through a sieve. Puree vegetables in a food processor and force through a sieve, adding to the roasting liquid. This is now the ultimate sauce for prime rib. Carve roast at the table and serve with ultimate sauce.

Chef Bob & Chef Kris (Peacock Alley Kitchen)

Smoked Beef Brisket

1 whole beef brisket

3 Tablespoons oil

4 Tablespoons beef rub (see index)

Rub brisket with oil and **beef rub (see index)**. Wrap in plastic wrap and refrigerate for 24 hours. Using a commercial smoker, follow manufacturer's instructions and smoke brisket for 4-5 hours at 250°. Use a flavored wood such as hickory or pecan. Low and slow is the secret.

Corn Bread Dressing

A Deep South side dish that is usually made on Sunday's, not just on Thanksgiving. There are many variations to this recipe with the addition of cooked pork sausage, or cooked and chopped oysters.

1 recipe of corn bread (crumbled)

1 onion (diced)

4 stalks celery (diced)

5 Tablespoons oil

4-6 cups chicken stock

1 cup cooked turkey meat (pulled or chopped)

1 Tablespoon rubbed sage

salt and pepper

5 eggs

Sauté onion and celery in oil until soft. Crumble corn bread in a large bowl, add onions and celery. Add all other ingredients and taste for salt and pepper. Put dressing into casserole dish and bake 30-40 minutes at 350°. Add cooked sausage or oysters before baking if desired.

Chicken in Dressing

The first time I had this dish I was having Sunday dinner with my future wife's family. There were bowls of mashed potatoes, peas, salad, biscuits, okra, butter beans, corn, and a huge pan of cornbread dressing. I asked where was the chicken and everybody laughed. It was their tradition to bake the chicken in the dressing. What a great flavor the dressing has and what immense taste and texture the chicken develops during cooking.

1 large roasting hen

1 cup kosher salt

¼ cup sugar

2 quarts water

1 carrot

1 onion

3 stalks celery

1 recipe cornbread dressing (doubled)

Wash chicken and rub with salt inside and out. Place in a pot large enough to hold the chicken, salt, sugar and water. Soak chicken in this brine approximately 12 hours, refrigerated. Remove chicken, drain and pat dry with paper towels. Salt and pepper chicken. Rough cut the celery, onion, and carrot. Stuff chicken with the vegetables. Double the corn bread dressing recipe, and in a large, deep roasting pan place the salt and peppered hen and cover with uncooked dressing. Bake at 350° for 1 1/2 to 2 hours until internal temperature of the bird is 165°.

What a wondrous and perfectly cooked surprise awaits the guests at the table.

BBQ Pork Butt

The Deep South is considered the masters of BBQ. Everyone has their own way of doing it, and to them it is the best way. This recipe is more technique rather than ingredients.

2 pork butts

1 cup BBQ spice

Rub pork with BBQ spice and let rest in refrigerator for 8-10 hours. Prepare smoker according to manufacturers instructions. Cook in smoker for 8-10 hours at 250° until meat is tender. Pull meat off bone and add **BBQ sauce and Chef Bob's Chow-Chow (see index).**

Roasted Turkey

Turkey is not just for the holidays. Turkey's are available year round. Pick out a young bird and thaw for 3 days in a refrigerator or in an ice chest for 12-15 hours, filled with water, changing twice daily. Drain and dry thawed turkey. Salt and pepper bird inside and out.

1 12-15 pound turkey (thawed)

1 onion (peeled)

1 carrot (broken in half)

1 stalk celery (broken in half)

1 sprig rosemary

1 bay leaf

2 cinnamon sticks

Remove turkey giblets and use for stock or **gravy (see index)**. Stuff salt and peppered bird with all ingredients. Bend wings back and place bird in a roasting pan. Cover with foil. Roast in 325° oven for approximately 3 to 3 1/2 hours, after 2 hours remove foil and cook 1 to 1 1/2 more hours or until internal temperature of thickest part of bird is 165°. DO NOT BASTE BIRD! This is a cooking misconception. Basting will actually dry out your bird.

Deep Fried Turkey

1 Whole turkey (10-15 pounds)

5 gallons oil (peanut oil preferred)

3 Tablespoons poultry rub

6 Tablespoons white wine

In a 40-60 quart pot with strainer, place turkey in the empty pot. Pour water over turkey until water covers turkey by 2 inches. Measure the watermark. This will be how much oil you will need. Remove turkey and dry with paper towels. Pour out water and dry pot completely. Fill pot with oil to the watermark. Place over a propane burner in a grassy or sandy area. Bring oil temperature to 360°. Wash and dry turkey. Mix poultry rub with white wine and use an injector to pump the turkey with this mixture. Follow injector manufacturer's instructions. Using the pot's frying strainer, lower the turkey (legs pointing into oil) slowly in the preheated oil. You may want to purchase some heat resistant gloves because the strainer handle gets very hot. Fry turkey for 3 minutes per pound. A 10 pound turkey will take 30 minutes. A 3 pound chicken should take 9 minutes. To be safe, use a meat thermometer and measure the temperature in the thickest part of the turkey or chicken. The temperature should be 165°. Slowly remove bird and allow excess oil to drain. Bird will stay hot about 1 hour.

Baked Ham

Pigs actually came from South America. Thank you South America. The Deep South is the ham-eating center of the world. I could probably write a book on ham, sausage and the like. This is a simple recipe, but will serve you well. The most important ingredient in this recipe is the ham itself. Ask your butcher for the best, bone in, shank end, smoked ham with the skin still on.

1 10-15 pound shank end smoked ham

1 cup Dijon mustard

1 pound brown sugar

1 Tablespoon kosher salt

Wash ham and cover with water in a sink or large pot. Soak for 1-2 hours. Rinse and dry ham. With a very sharp knife slice 1 inch deep cuts into skin from bone end to bone end at a 45 degree angle. Turn ham and cut again in the opposite direction, creating a diamond pattern. The diamond pattern is for show, but the cuts are to allow water and fat to drain during cooking. Place ham on a roasting rack in a roasting pan. Place in a 400° oven for 45 minutes to 1 hour. Remove ham and cut away skin. This is called cracklings, chopped and used in corn bread named cracklin' bread. Paint mustard on ham with a pastry brush. Pack on dry brown sugar. Sprinkle with kosher salt. Place back in oven for 1 to 1 1/2 hours. Allow to cool for 30 minutes to one hour before carving. Carve toward the bone in thin slices, including the sugar crust. Serve with **sweet potato casserole** or **sweet potato cress (see index)**.

Sister Sarah's Salmon Patties

Being a chef and restaurant owner, it is so comforting to have someone who loves your family as much as our sweet, dear Sarah. During the busiest restaurant months she will bring to our house, platters of salmon patties, 12 inch rounds of cornbread, fresh green beans, and gallons of sweetened iced tea. All to keep us from having to cook again. This recipe is a tribute to Sarah, our beautiful, spiritual mother. Thank you for all the great home cooked meals.

6 cups of cooked and crumbled salmon

2 boiled and cooled potatoes (grated on a box grater)

1 onion (grated on a box grater)

5 tablespoons plain flour

4 eggs

1 stick melted butter

1 Tablespoon chopped dill

juice from 1 lemon

salt and pepper to taste

1 stick butter for browning patties

1 cup of seasoned flour

Combine all ingredients in a mixing bowl. Chill for 1 hour, then shape into patties or little cakes. Dust with seasoned flour and brown in butter. Keep warm in 200° oven.

Oyster Bake

In Gulf Shores and Apalachicola Alabama there is no shortage of oysters. Oyster bakes in Alabama are as common as clam bakes in Maine. The oysters are dumped on top of hot coals and covered with damp burlap sacks. You can recreate this taste on your own grill. Preferably over a wood grill, place oysters on grill grates and cover with grill lid. Allow to bake until oyster opens. The oysters will not open like clams do, but will give you an easy time of opening the jewel of the sea. For a more elaborate baked oyster, follow my recipe for Baked half shells.

Baked Half Shells

24 clean oyster shells (or more)

1 pint fresh shucked oysters (or frozen, thawed)

1 small onion diced fine

4 cloves garlic chopped

1 stalk celery diced fine

3-4 pieces smoked bacon diced

3 lemons juiced

1 cup toasted bread crumbs

1/2 stick melted butter

2 tablespoons chopped parsley

Begin cooking diced bacon in a non-stick skillet. When most of the fat has rendered, add onion, garlic, and celery. Sauté until vegetables are softened. Remove from heat and allow to cool. Place clean half shells on a baking sheet. Deposit 1 oyster in each shell, then spoon lemon juice over oysters and distribute vegetable topping evenly over the top of every oyster. Mix breadcrumbs with melted butter and parsley, sprinkle over each lovely oyster. Bake in 350° oven for 20 minutes. Great appetizer.

Oysters Florentine

A classic dish from the 1800's. Very French and a great appetizer. I have probably made over 50,000 of these beauties.

1 pound fresh spinach

3 cloves garlic chopped

1 shallot sliced thin

2-3 Tablespoons olive oil

3-4 Tablespoons sherry (or white wine)

1 pint shucked oysters

24 cleaned oyster shell

3 Tablespoons grated Parmesan cheese

½ cup heavy cream

½ cheese sauce recipe (see index)

Sauté shallots and garlic in oil. Add spinach and begin cooking. Add sherry and cream. Cook for 2-3 minutes, set aside to cool. Place some of the creamed spinach in each oyster shell. Place an oyster on top of the spinach. Spoon a small amount of **cheese sauce (see index)** over oyster, then sprinkle with Parmesan and bake in a 400° oven until browned.

Sir Robert "Chef Bob" Vaningan O.S.C.

Crab Cakes

I always think of McGregor's tavern in Annapolis, Maryland when I make crab cakes.

This place is famous for its crab cakes. People line up out the door on weekends just to get the crab cake sandwich. I took that experience, and a quick crab cake lesson from a guy named Kris at the Waldorf-Astoria and came up with this simple, yet perfect crab cake. When you eat a crab cake, you should taste crab, not bread or bell peppers or anything else. This recipe has no onions, peppers or garlic, just crab and a thick milk gravy. Make sure to use jumbo lump and smell the crabmeat. It should smell like a clean ocean breeze.

1 cup milk

5 Tablespoons butter

5 Tablespoons flour

1/2 teaspoon salt

1/8 teaspoon cayenne pepper

3 egg yolks

2 pounds jumbo lump crabmeat

bread crumbs (Japanese preferred)

oil for frying (peanut oil preferred)

Melt butter and whisk in flour and cook for 2-3 minutes. Add milk, salt and pepper. Bring to a boil, stirring continuously. It should be very thick. Allow to cool, fold in crab. Portion into equal parts and make a small patty. Coat generously with bread crumbs, and using a cookie cutter or portion ring, place crumb coated cake in ring, then squeeze to pack the cake tight, using extra bread crumbs to prevent sticking. Deep fry in hot oil 350° for 1-2 minutes just to brown. Drain on paper towels. When ready to serve the crab cakes, place them in the oven at 400° for 15 minutes. Serve with **tartar sauce (see index)** enhanced with Dijon mustard. WOW!

Papa John on the coast

Deep-South Fried Chicken

I worked with a sweet, older lady named Miss Ruby. Her fried chicken was the best I have ever tasted. When I asked her to teach me, she showed me step by step and said, "It aint nuttin' but salt, pepper, and a little paprika baby." I tried, but it never came out as good as hers. Perhaps it was because she had raised, plucked and fried over 10,000 chickens in her lifetime, or maybe it was the way she breaded the chicken with her beautiful, black, leather like, hands. It could have been how her mother taught her. Perhaps the pleasure of eating Miss Ruby's fried chicken should be only a memory that makes me smile, and makes me sad at the same time, since Miss Ruby has passed on to a spiritual life now. I think this recipe will serve you well. A deep iron pot will help make you successful. A large iron skillet will work as well. Careful not to use a skillet too small, the oil will overflow.

1 frying chicken cut into pieces

6 cups plain flour

3 Tablespoons paprika

3 Tablespoons black pepper

1 Tablespoon salt

5 cups oil (peanut oil preferred)

4 Tablespoons poultry rub

8 eggs

Wash and dry chicken. Rub chicken with poultry rub. Mix flour, paprika, salt, and pepper. Divide into two medium bowls. Whisk eggs in a large bowl. Roll chicken in seasoned flour. Pat excess flour off, then dip chicken into eggs. Roll chicken in the second flour mixture, coating chicken thoroughly. Heat oil in a very large cast iron pot or skillet to 350°. Fry chicken for 12 minutes. Larger pieces may need two to three more minutes. Check for doneness with a thermometer that should read 165° inserted into the thickest part of the piece you are testing. Heat oven to 300°. As chicken comes out of fryer, drain on wire rack. Place fried chicken in oven while you finish frying the rest of the chicken pieces.

Georgian Quail (stuffed) with Blackeyed Peas

Grilled Georgian Quail

Georgia has some of the best quail farms in America. Southern quail are fat and very tasty. This recipe works with other small game birds as well. If possible, buy quail and other game birds semi boned. You can do this yourself with some practice.

4 Quail semi boned

1 pint blue berries

1 stick butter

salt and pepper

Salt and pepper quail inside and out. Melt butter, puree blueberries and mix together. Rub quail inside and out with blueberry mixture. Allow to marinate for at least 6 hours. Grill quail over medium high flames for 3 minutes per side. Heat leftover marinade to a boil and use as a sauce.

Fried Catfish

Fried catfish is one of the wonderful foods of the Deep South. In the south, when you order a fried catfish sandwich, make sure you order filet of catfish or you will get a whole fried baby catfish between 2 thick slices of white bread and a whole pickled hot pepper. Mississippi is the most famous for its abundance of catfish producers. Farm raised catfish is firm and very flaky. Use peanut oil to make this recipe. DON'T FORGET THE **HUSHPUPPIES! (see index)**

6 to 8 catfish filets

1 cup flour

salt and pepper to season the flour

2 cups buttermilk

2 eggs

1 cup fine cracker meal

1 cup corn meal (plain)

4 cups peanut oil

seasoned salt

Season the flour. Mix the buttermilk and the eggs in a separate container. Mix the cracker meal corn meal and seasoned salt (to taste) in a separate container. Heat oil to 350°. Dip filets in the seasoned flour. Shake off excess flour. Dip floured filets into the buttermilk and egg mixture, roll into cracker meal mixture, coating heavily. Now carefully lower into hot oil and cook for 3 to 5 minutes. Drain hot fish on a wire rack. When the fish comes out of the hot oil, sprinkle with a little seasoned salt.

Fried Catfish

Pig Ears and Tails

There is a tradition in the Deep-South of eating pig ears (flapper steaks) and tails. When I first heard of this as a teenaged boy I wondered why anyone would eat such a thing. I learned it wasn't because ears and tails had great flavor or lots of nutrition, but it is out of respect and love of generations of African slaves who were given ears, tails and pig's feet to make food for them selves. The respectful love and remembrance is like that of the Jewish Seder. What a humbling honor to be asked to partake of such a feast. Chitterlings, snout, and souse, are more examples of celebration soul foods you find in every grocery store in the Deep South.

2 quarts water

6 pig ears

6 pig tails

1 onion (diced)

3 pieces bacon (diced)

6 Tablespoons sugar

3 Tablespoons kosher salt

6 Tablespoons vinegar

1 Tablespoon black pepper

2 bunches turnip greens

Sauté' bacon and onion together until soft. Add sugar, salt, vinegar and pepper. Add water and bring to a boil. Add cleaned ears and tails. Simmer for 1 to 1 1/2 hours. Remove ears and tails to a platter. Use this pot of flavored water to cook turnip greens. Clean and prepare greens as in **Turnip Greens (see index)** recipe. Add cooked ears and tails back in the pot when greens are tender.

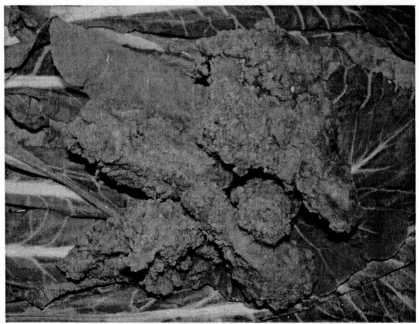

Fried Chicken

Braised Pig Feets

The French have been using pig's feet in recipes forever. One of the finest restaurants in Manhattan, New York, (Payard's Pastry and Bistro) has pig's feet on the menu. Pig feet are so common in the Deep-South, every store has fresh feet available. I spelled this recipe <u>feets</u> on purpose. Jeff "Bad Foots" Johnson refers to pig's feet as (pig feets). If you are not sure you can take the thought of whole pig's feet, buy pig shanks and you will have the same results. Don't knock it till you try it.

2 pig's feet split

2 cups flour

2 teaspoons salt

1 teaspoon pepper

1/2 cup oil

1 onion (chopped)

2 stalks celery (chopped)

2 carrots (peeled and chopped)

1 whole head of garlic (unpeeled and intact)

2 sprigs rosemary

2 sprigs thyme

2 bay leaves

1/2 bottle red wine

1 quart of water or stock or more if needed

Mix salt and pepper with flour. Dredge feet in flour and brown in hot oil. Remove feet from oil and set aside. Cook onions, celery, and carrots in oil until browned. Add red wine and scrape the goodie (browned particles on bottom of pot.) Add everything into pot. Bring to a boil and stir well. Turn off heat and cover with loose fitting lid. Place in center rack of oven at 250° for 6 to 8 hours, or until meat is very tender. Serve over mashed potatoes.

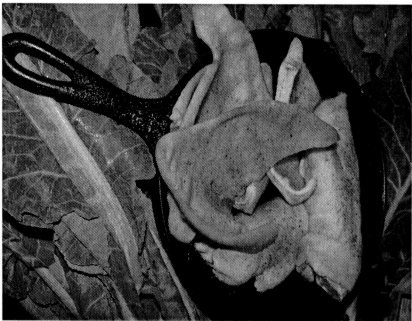

Pig's Ear and Pig's Feet ready to cook

Epilogue

The Deep-South has brought us soul food for reflection, nourishment, and remembrance. I am glad I was born in the Deep-South. With everyone around me serving one another with the labor of love, I found my GOD given gift of cooking. You should find your passion and use it to serve others. Examine your life and ask yourself, "What makes me passionate? What moves me emotionally?" What ever your answer is, that is your GOD given talent and it is the way you should make your living, or at least how you should spend your time. This life is a blink compared to the infinite Universe. My life and yours should be in constant communication with our Creator. We didn't evolve by accident. We have a mind, a body, and a spirit. If our spirit is weak, our mind and body will also be weak. The way to strengthen your spirit is by prayer and hearing the Word of GOD. First, ask the Lord for forgiveness of your sins, and to come into your heart to become Lord of your life. **Praying out loud, repeat these words: Jesus, forgive me, Lord. I am nothing without you. Come into my life and save me. I believe you are the son of GOD and only you can wash away my sins. You were born of a virgin. You were crucified for my sins, died and was buried. On the third day you rose again and accended to GOD the father to sit at HIS right hand. You will come again to receive us unto yourself. Thank you Lord for saving me. I love you.** If you prayed this prayer, according to the **Holy Bible** your name has been written in the Lamb's book of life. Now you can proceed with building your spirit with the Word of GOD and prayer. Since September 11, 2001 most people are more sensitive about how short our lives can be. We should love people as we would like to be loved by people. Keep these thoughts with you as you cook for someone or eat with someone. When you eat with someone it is a very special time. You are making a commitment to love that person as you love yourself. This is what life is all about, for us to help each other get to that spiritual place we are all waiting to see. Food is a large part of that mission. Shalom! Peace be with you and, may His face shine upon you and give you peace, may you be healed from the top of your head to the souls of your feet, and may

Sir Robert "Chef Bob" Vaningan O.S.C.

the Angels guard you and keep you safe from all harm. Amen. Sir
Robert Vaningan O.S.C

Chef Bob's favorite web sites and books

www.ruhlman.com
www.danielnyc.com
www.altmarkphoto.com
www.jfolse.com
www.mustardseedfoods.com
www.pastrychef.com
www.jbprince.com
www.pattycakes.com
www.petergabriel.com
www.grits.com
www.sangelatocafe.com
www.leshalles.net
www.babbonyc.com
www.triggerstreet.com
www.cgourmet.com
www.exit4.net
www.mrchocolate.com
www.payard.com
www.1stbooks.com
www.efood-source.net

Trap lines North by Stephen W. Meader
New American Classics by Jeremiah Tower
Kitchen Confidential by Anthony Bourdain
The Soul of a Chef by Michael Ruhlman
The Frugal Gourmet Keeps the Feast by Jeff Smith
The New Larousse Gastronomique by Auguste Escoffier &
Phileas Gilbert
The Modern Patissier by William Barker
Le Repertoire de la Cusine by l.Saulnier
The Escoffier Cook Book by A. Escoffier
Beard on Breads by James Beard
Cooking with Daniel Boulud by Daniel Boulud
Dessert Circus by Jacque Torres

Sir Robert "Chef Bob" Vaningan O.S.C.

Simply Sensational Desserts by Francios Payard
Plantation Celebrations by John Folse
A Treasury of Southern Baking by Prudence Hillburn

Index

Sir Robert "Chef Bob" Vaningan O.S.C.

About the Author

www.chefbob.com

Chef Bob Vaningan O.S.C. is the owner /operator of Chef Bob & Company Catering since 1996. He is also the creator of The Chocolate Cottage and a regular guest Chef on Fox 6's "Good Day Alabama Show," since 1997, a member of the American Culinary Federation since 1986, and an active participant in fund raisers for the Alabama Symphony, American Cancer Society, The Salvation Army, and the American Liver Foundation. Chef Bob directed a team of Chefs twice, for the Admiral of the United States Naval Academy in Annapolis, Maryland. His team produced the Navy's 220th birthday party for the Secretary of the Navy, the Chief of Naval Operations and 300 distinguished alumni. This trip also included a private (behind the scenes) tour of the White House, with an invitation to return. In June 1995, Chef Bob served as Guest Chef to New York City's Waldorf-Astoria "Peacock Alley Restaurant." While in New York, Chef Bob also served as Guest Chef to Daniel Boulud, Francios Payard, Jacques Torres, Claude Trigros, Henry Meer & Laurent Manrique. Chef Bob was Knighted Sir Robert "Chef Bob" Vaningan, to the Order of Saint Catherine as a Royal Chef of the House d' Anjou of France by His Most Eminent Royal Highness, Prince Dolgrouky d' Anjou, Prince Regent of the House d' Anjou of France. Chef Bob's American Culinary Awards include: Two Bronze medals, presented in Chicago for World Class Cooking Competitions; one Silver medal for Most Original Presentation; and one Bronze for Mystery Basket competition. Chef Bob is also adept in Marzipan modeling, Pastillage, Gum Paste, and Ice Sculpture. He is dedicated to teaching all that he has learned in his culinary life. "I believe I have a God-given talent for cooking," says Chef Bob, "and I love it with a Passion. In my opinion, to excel as a cook, Passion is the main ingredient."

Printed in the United States
1089800002B/61-258